Recessions

VOLUME I

Brian Romanchuk

Published by BondEconomics, Canada

www.BondEconomics.com

Published by BondEconomics, 2020, Montréal Québec.

Nothing in this book constitutes investment or tax advice. Investors are advised to seek professional advice tailored to their situation. Although best efforts have been made to ensure the validity of information contained herein, there is no guarantee of its accuracy or completeness.

Library and Archives Canada

Recessions: Volume I

Brian Romanchuk 1968-

ISBN 978-1-7751676-6-2 Epub Edition

ISBN 978-1-7751676-5-5 Kindle Edition

ISBN 978-1-7751676-7-9 Paperback Edition

Contents

Acknowledgements

I would like to thank the readers of my articles at BondEconomics.com for their feedback. Portions of this text previously appeared as articles on that site, and I have been able to incorporate suggestions and corrections.I would also like to thank Judy Yelon for her editing of this text.

Finally, any errors and omissions are my own.

Chapter 1 **Overview**

1.1 Introduction

Recessions (and their larger siblings, depressions) are a recurring feature of industrial capitalism. Quite often associated with financial crises, they are disruptive to workers as well as financial markets. From the perspective of fixed income practitioners, they usually trigger substantial volatility in the interest rate cycle, as central banks typically cut rates rapidly to restart growth.

This book looks at the theory of recessions from a (mainly) post-Keynesian perspective. What are the mechanisms behind recessions, and what do various theories or models predict?

This volume is what might be described as a "guided survey": there is a theoretical narrative, but it is developed by surveying existing theories. The writing style is at an intermediate level, being at about the same complexity as what might be seen in the business press, but with a large body of footnotes/endnotes to point readers to academic papers. Existing academic survey papers are leaned on heavily, giving a starting point for literature surveys by readers. Real-world data and simulation results are used to illustrate points; only a few elementary equations appear.

The main theoretical argument is that recessions are inherently hard to forecast. Anyone who has read financial market commentary for an extended period will not be surprised by this; missed recession calls are a pervasive phenomenon. The interesting question is: why are recessions hard to forecast? The mechanisms outlined in this book help explain why theory suggests that this should be so.

In addition to a focus on theory, there is a chapter on empirical recession models. These are models that take economic and financial time series and are used to generate recession forecasts. Since these are algorithms that operate on time series data, they are not closely tied to any theoretical model of how the economy works. The models surveyed were largely generated by economists who would be considered mainstream, and so one might not view this volume as purely post-Keynesian.

The second volume will widen the topics covered and provide an overview of mainstream (neoclassical) business cycle theory. This will allow a comparison of the competing theories versus observed data.

This book was written before the economic contraction triggered by the Pandemic of 2020 occurred. Other than a few notes to reflect the events, it is not discussed. The second volume will discuss the events, aided by the arrival of data, as well as the added perspective provided by the theoretical discussions that are deferred to Volume II.

1.2   What is a Recession?

The first challenge in discussing recessions is defining what exactly a recession is. One rule of thumb is that a recession is anytime there are two consecutive quarters of declining real gross domestic product (GDP). Although I use the "two consecutive quarters of declining GDP" definition for some countries (as discussed in the next section), we probably want to work with a different definition.

(In case the reader is unfamiliar with the concept of GDP, it is the total value of goods and services produced in the domestic economy. It does not count every single transaction, like the resale of goods between wholesalers and retailers, nor financial transactions. Nominal GDP is the value of domestic production in current dollar terms and is equal to nominal domestic income. Real GDP – which is what is used in the recession definition – adjusts nominal GDP to remove the effect of inflation. In a high inflation environment, nominal GDP might not decline in a recession.)

NBER Recession Definition

In the United States, the National Bureau of Economic Research (NBER) has a business cycle dating committee that makes determinations of the start and end months of recessions. (The fact that they work with a monthly frequency is valuable for recession dating, as recessions tend to be short-lived.)

The NBER has a brief qualitative description of their methodology on their website: https://www.nber.org/cycles/recessions.html. They write:

> *The NBER's Business Cycle Dating Committee maintains a chronology of the U.S. business cycle. The chronology comprises alternating dates of peaks and troughs in economic activity. A recession is a period between a peak and a trough, and an expansion is a period between a trough and a peak. During a recession, a significant decline in economic activity spreads across the economy and can last from a few months to more than a year. Similarly, during an expansion, economic activity rises substantially, spreads across the economy, and usually lasts for several years.*

The definition refers to "economic activity." One way of expressing that concept is the level of real GDP, hence there is an overlap with the "two consecutive quarters of declining GDP." However, the NBER Business Cycle Dating Committee uses a broader definition of activity.

The Committee does not have a fixed definition of economic activity. It examines and compares the behavior of various measures of broad activity: real GDP measured on the product and income sides, economy-wide employment, and real income. The Committee also may consider indicators that do not cover the entire economy, such as real sales and the Federal Reserve's index of industrial production (IP). The Committee's use of these indicators in conjunction with the broad measures recognizes the issue of double-counting of sectors included in both those indicators and the broad measures. Still, a well-defined peak or trough in real sales or IP might help to determine the overall peak or trough dates, particularly if the economy-wide indicators are in conflict or do not have well-defined peaks or troughs.

By using other indicators, it is possible to fix start and end months. It also avoids some concerns with real GDP. For example, GDP included imputed measures of value-added, which will not rise and fall with the business cycle.

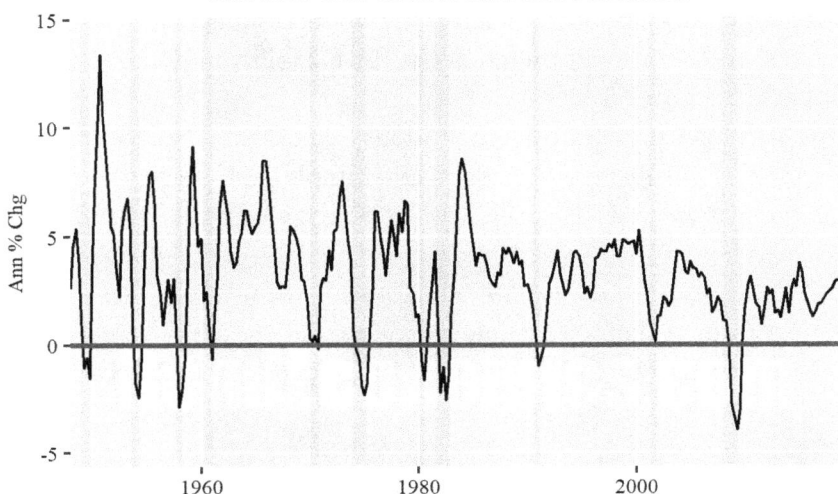

U.S. Real GDP Growth Rate And Recessions*

*NBER definition. Source: BEA (via FRED).

U.S Real GDP and recessions

The previous chart shows the post-1949 history of real GDP growth and recessions. The annual percentage change in real GDP is depicted, with the recession periods in the United States (as defined by the NBER committee) shaded in pink. As expected, growth rates fell in recessionary periods. One thing to note is that showing the annual percentage change, we are comparing real GDP in a quarter with its level four quarters earlier. This smooths out the wiggles in quarterly data. One side effect is that the growth rate (on this measure) remained positive throughout the 2001 recession, while real GDP shrank in the first and third quarter of 2001 (using the current measure of GDP, which may be revised in the future as a result of changes to definitions). Since the shrinkage did not occur in consecutive quarters, this recession would not qualify under the "two consecutive quarters of declining real GDP" definition.

Definitions Vary Across Countries

For the United States, the National Bureau of Economic Research (NBER) has managed to become the authoritative source for recession dating, whereas for other countries, recession dating determination is less clear. In this text, I stick with the NBER definition for the United States and treat other countries on a case-by-case basis. In my figures, I indicate what method is used to generate the recession bars. Since I think we should be more concerned about the side-effects of recessions than formal declarations of recessions, my preference is for flexibility in definition. (I return to this in Section 2.5.)

Rather than attempt to list the various bodies that date recessions in other regions, I will just use Canada as an example. In Canada, the C.D. Howe Institute has created a Business Cycle Council which has a mandate to date recessions: https://www.cdhowe.org/council/business-cycle-council. The next figure shows the post-1990 history of real GDP growth and the recession dates as defined by that committee. There are two declared recessionary periods: March 1990 to April 1992, and October 2008 to May 2009.

Canadian Real GDP And Recessions*

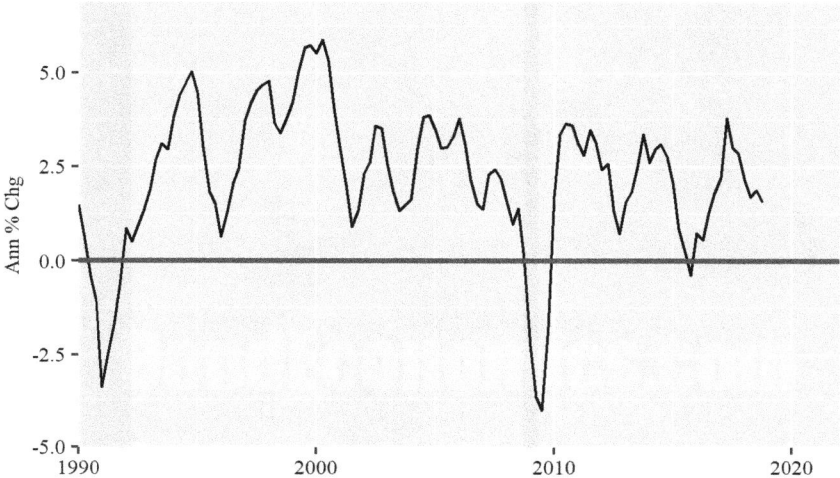

*C.D. Howe Business Cycle Council. Source: OECD (via DB.nomics).

Canadian real GDP growth

Considerable Leeway in Definitions

From a practical perspective, one might argue that the bar used by the C.D. Howe committee for declaring a recession is too high.

The top panel of the next figure shows the Canadian unemployment rate and the C.D. Howe Business Cycle Council's recession dates. (Note that this council was formed after the 2008 Financial Crisis, and so the earlier recession dates were based on applying academics' methodologies to past data.) The unemployment rate rose by just over 1% in 2001, in a relatively rapid fashion. Although the downturn was somewhat localised, it certainly felt like a depression for anyone associated with the technology industry.

Canadian Unemploment Rate And Recessions*

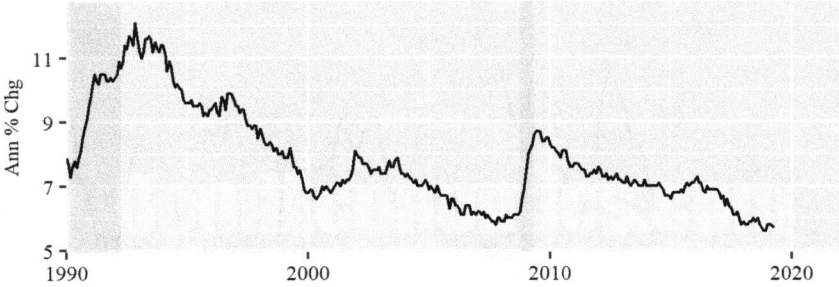

Canadian Rise In Unemployment Rate And Recessions*

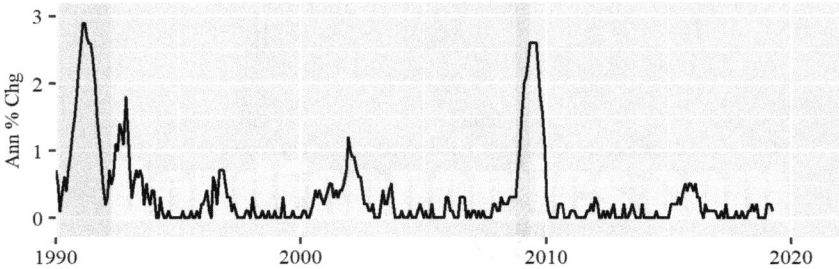

*C.D. Howe Business Cycle Council. Source: Statscan.

Canadian unemployment rate and recessions

The bottom panel shows the rise in unemployment rate versus the trailing minimum value over the past 12 months (including the current month, so the minimum of this time series is zero). We see a big jump in 1992, as well as 2001, that were not classified as recessions (based on continued growth in other economic activity series).

I would argue that the rise in the unemployment rate over-shadows the other activity indicators for two sets of reasons.

- **Normative policy perspective.** We should react to a rise in the unemployment rate based on ethics, as well as the cost to society created by unemployment, as well as the long-lasting effects of job loss (referred to as "hysteresis").

- **Inflation-targeting perspective.** In the post-1990 environment, the only plausible candidate for "capacity constraints" in the do-mestic developed economies revolves around the labour market – rather than the commodity markets. There is a massive excess of manufacturing and service sector productive capacity, so that growth in output alone is not enough to trigger a plausible inflation risk. (Note that although I view NAIRU to be a questionable concept, I accept that labour market "tightening" (vaguely defined) will eventually pose wage inflation risks. As we have discovered repeatedly since the 1990s, an unemployment rate that is drifting lower tells us little about inflation risks, but a rapid rise probably is telling us something.)

Canadian Target Rate And Recessions*

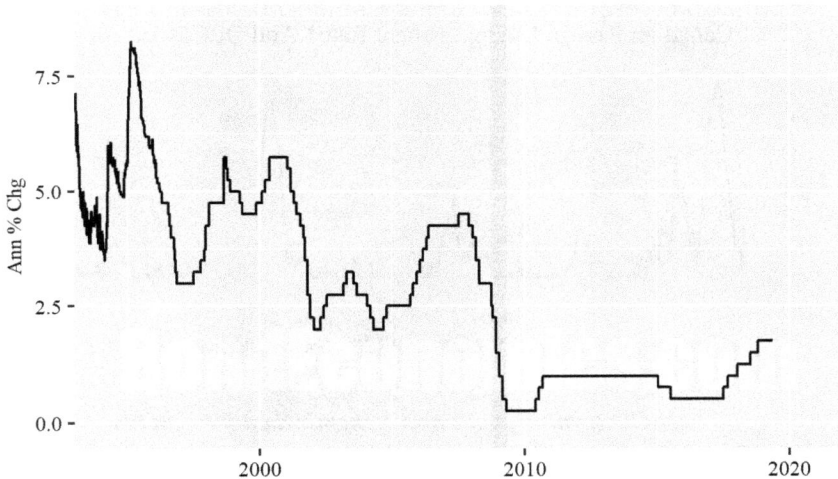

*C.D. Howe. Source: Bank of Canada via Statscan.

Canadian policy rate and recessions

My comments here on the importance of the rise in the unemployment rate are not purely my opinions: the Bank of Canada reacted to the weakness in the labour market (chart above). From a bond market participant's perspective, the drop in the target rate from 5.75% in January 2001 to 2% in 2002 is what you are paid to forecast, not what the C.D. Howe Business Cycle Council thinks.

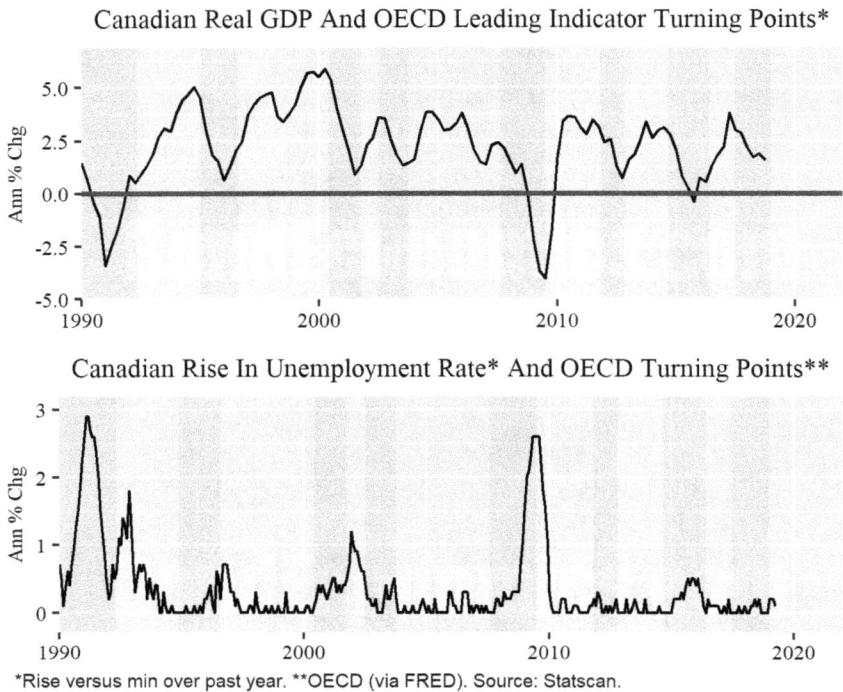

Canadian Real GDP And OECD Leading Indicator Turning Points*

Canadian Rise In Unemployment Rate* And OECD Turning Points**

*Rise versus min over past year. **OECD (via FRED). Source: Statscan.

OECD turning points and economic data for Canada
However, it is possible to get a definition that is perhaps too sensitive
to economic fluctuations. The figure above shows Canadian real GDP,
and the "turning points" defined by the OECD leading economic indicator. (URL: http://www.oecd.org/sdd/leading-indicators/oecdcompos-
iteleadingindicatorsreferenceturningpointsandcomponentseries.htm.) The
OECD has these indicators for most (if not all) of the countries in their
data coverage universe.

The shaded regions show where the OECD leading economic indicator
dropped from a local peak to a local trough. It does align very well with
the acceleration and deceleration of real GDP growth, so these indicators
could be useful for some purposes. (For example, financial markets might
be sensitive to such acceleration.)

However, the "negative turning points" appear to be too numerous to
be taken as a definition of a recession. For example, we saw very little in
the way of a rise in the unemployment rate during two of the episodes after 2010, and only about 0.5% in the third (bottom panel) – although that

0.5 rise would have breached the trigger proposed by Sahm (Section 2.5).

Is There a "Best" Dating Methodology?

My interest here is in the theory of relatively deep recessions. They do not have to be as devastating as the crisis in 2008 but need to be deeper than the fluctuations that seem to be captured by the OECD indicators. The reason is straightforward: these big dips in activity typically result in large errors in economic forecasts, which is my theoretical preoccupation.

As a result, I have a primarily qualitative interest in recessions, and do not see much value in trying to find the "best" recession-dating methodology. Instead, I argue that we might be interested in different aspects of recessions and we might need a different set of criteria for each aspect. In the United States, the NBER-defined recession dates have done a very good job of coinciding with most aspects of interest, but the experience in other countries seems to be somewhat more muddled (as in the Canadian post-2010 experience), and so recession dating is going to be more controversial.

1.3 Are Recessions Forecastable?

Recessions are of interest for both practical and theoretical reasons. From a practical perspective, calling for a recession when the consensus is for steady growth is a sure way to get attention. From the perspective of theory, recessions are where we can determine the relative usefulness of economic theories. During an expansion, economies are characterised by steady growth, and it is hard to distinguish between models that can generate trending behaviour (with relatively small deviations, or "noise"). Recessions are when the interesting dynamics happens. (The tendency for economic volatility to be clustered around recessions is itself an interesting feature of the data.)

Being able to fit a story to a historical recession is interesting, but of limited usefulness. Any number of stories can be told about the data; one only needs to look at the never-ending debates between economic bulls and bears in financial market commentary to see that it is possible to fit any number of theories against observed data. What we want to be able to do is forecast future recessions.

Recessions are a Generic Event

The first challenge to forecasting is that recessions are a generic economic event. For simplicity, let us use the simplest standard for defining a recession: two consecutive quarters of declining real gross domestic product (GDP) growth. Gross domestic product is an aggregate concept and is the sum of a number of components. A decline in real GDP represents a decline in one or more of those components, and the reason why each component may decline can easily be different.

We can use an analogy from physics (since everyone loves using physics for analogies for economics). Let us assume that the event of interest is a body moving from point A to point B. This can happen for any number of reasons.

- The body is self-propelled, like a car or a kitten.
- The body has metal components that are attracted by a magnet.
- The body has an electric charge and is embedded in an electric field.

Newton's law of motion will describe the dynamics of the move from point A to point B, but the explanation of *why* the movement occurred lies in some other fundamental physical laws.

Multiple Causes of Recessions

Returning to recession forecasting, we do face a multiplicity of potential causes for recessions; forecasting whether the economy will be in recession implies being able to forecast one or possibly all those potential factors.

For example, there is a consensus that tightening fiscal policy sufficiently will cause a recession. ("Tightening fiscal policy" is the act of raising tax rates and/or cutting government spending.) Admittedly, there are some free market leaning economists who appear to disagree with the assessment that fiscal policy can cause a recession, but I am unsure how serious those objections are. (The usual argument is framed as follows: a fiscal stimulus cannot cause faster growth. The possibility of fiscal policy going in the other direction is not examined, since the concern is to downplay the possibility that government intervention can raise growth rates.) There is also the related idea of "expansionary austerity," which suggests that moderate fiscal tightening will not cause a recession. I discuss expansionary austerity in Section 3.4. The usual description is that the fiscal tightening is done in a controlled fashion, and so this does not rule out the possibility that a drastic fiscal tightening causes a recession, and so proponents of expansionary austerity do not necessarily fall outside what I refer to as the consensus view.

If we accept that tight fiscal policy can cause a recession, one aspect of recession forecasting is political forecasting: will the government enact such a policy on the forecast horizon? Although one would need economic models to assess the expected effects of the policy change, whether the policy will be enacted is outside the bounds of standard economic theory. This will be discussed at greater length in Chapter 3.

Although we may face multiple possible causes of recessions, we can still narrow down discussion to an interesting class: recessions caused by disruptions in debt dynamics. For example, the deep global recession associated with the Financial Crisis that peaked in 2008 was a sterling example of disruption in debt markets.

Why are Recessions Hard to Forecast?

My argument is that recessions related to credit market disruptions are inherently hard to forecast. In particular, I do not expect that these recessions can be forecast using mathematical economic models (econometric models).[1]

I do not view that claim as being novel from the standpoint of academic economics, rather it is my interpretation of existing post-Keynesian theory. However, the ways in which the logic has been expressed are often not clear to outsiders.

I summarise the logic of the argument as follows.

1. An interesting and important class of recessions is caused by the disruption of investment (or even consumption) in the private sector that coincides with a decline in borrowing flows.
2. In modern capitalist societies, lending decisions end up being *de facto* centralised because of the institutional structure.
3. Forecasting such recessions described in point (1) is an analytical exercise that is equivalent to being able to forecast accurately the price movements of credit markets (using market jargon, directional credit forecasts).

1   I am assuming that the forecast horizon is relatively long, like six months. It might be possible to forecast a near-run recession, such as a recession starting next month. Various economic time series are slow-moving enough that certain conditions might reliably occur just ahead of a formal recession start date.

4. To the extent that the reader believes a loose version of the Efficient Markets Hypothesis – that market direction is impossible to forecast – quantitative recession forecasting is similarly impossible.

To make my stance clear – I am not saying that recession forecasting is impossible, rather that you would also have to be able to perform a far more lucrative analytical exercise, which is being an amazing credit market forecaster.

Another point to keep in mind is that I am referring to *unconditional forecasts*, a forecast that is a statement that some event will happen in the future. *Conditional forecasting* is an alternative strategy: an event X will happen if condition Y occurs. For example, forecasting a recession if tax rates are hiked by 30%, or if there is a mass default event, is entirely plausible. The problem is that we are replacing the problem of forecasting the recession with the problem of forecasting the preceding condition (in my examples, the tax hike or mass default). My belief is that conditional forecasting is the most useful strategy, but it is unsatisfying since we need to forecast conditions correctly. (From an investing standpoint, conditional forecasting is the preferred strategy, as we can attempt to implement a portfolio structure that performs well under what we see as the most likely outcomes, while limiting losses in adverse scenarios.)

As a final technical point, when I refer to "credit markets," I am not referring to just public markets in bonds and money market instruments (and associated products dreamed up by investment bankers). I am including traditional bank finance as part of the credit markets, even though bank lending decisions appear opaque and are not mark-to-market (thus some commentators treat bank lending as a different animal). The dividing line between banks and non-bank financial entities is typically blurry in practice, now that regulatory regimes no longer enforce strict operating procedure differences (like the Canadian "four-pillar structure," which split chartered banks, insurance companies, trust companies, and investment dealers). Some genres of economic models treat banks as completely distinct entities from bond markets, and there is a mythology around bank money creation.[2] This mythology blurs the reality that the economic per-

---

2   My book *Abolish Money (From Economics)!* discusses the misleading effects of the mythology around money and banking in economics.

spectives on lending decisions are very similar for bank and non-bank institutions – and so a credit freeze will tend to hit all forms of lending at the same time.

Roadmap for the Rest of the Text

The previous discussion laid out the theoretical roadmap of where we want to go. However, we need to do the theoretical work needed to get there. This first volume lays out the fundamentals of post-Keynesian theory around recessions. The second volume will deal with more advanced topics. This background should then make the previous set of assertions more plausible to the reader.

1.4   About this Book

This is the first volume of a two-volume work. This section now describes some of the features of the first volume, and then moves to a discussion of the second.

First Volume

This volume offers a survey of the theory of recessions, from a post-Keynesian (or "heterodox") perspective. There is very little in the way of mathematics, although the text refers to mathematical models. (The models themselves are implemented as code, see below.) Some technical digressions may only make sense to more advanced readers, but the author hopes that these will not be too discouraging for other readers.

This text is what I call an intermediate level: slightly more advanced than the writing in the business press, but not at the level of an academic paper. My objective is to provide a good overview of the subject that would allow a reader to then understand more advanced research.

Rather than use a bibliography – which is inconvenient for electronic book readers – I cite papers in either endnotes or footnotes (depending upon the book edition). Although I am surveying the field, I am writing a popularisation, not an academic survey. I will typically only refer to one or two papers in each section as examples of research in the field but will discuss them at length. As an ex-academic, I understand the sensitivity to claims about priority of research. I do not have access to a research library (nor the inclination) to make definitive judgements regarding who is first associated with research claims that I refer to here. The audience who is interested in such claims – academics – should have the capacity to make such judgements themselves. The "Further Reading" section of the book gives the bibliographic information for books that are referred to multiple times within the text.

The charts of economic analysis were prepared using the Python and R programming languages, with the code in the open source *econ_platform* package.[3] The *econ_platform* code downloads both the time series history and series metadata, so the analysis package is essentially self-documenting. I present the results of some stock-flow consistent (SFC) models. I do not include the mathematical description of these models, rather the Python code that generates them is available as part of the open source *sfc_models* package.[4]

Second Volume

At the time of writing, the second volume was not completed, as there were still research topics to explore. As a result, comments on the second volume's contents are tentative.

The following are the main subjects covered in the second volume.

- Neoclassical ("mainstream") *theory* will be introduced and discussed. (My discussion of empirical analysis of recessions in this volume is largely from mainstream authors; however, these results are not tied to neoclassical theory.) I have attempted to avoid digressions critiquing neoclassical theory, which I feel is a weakness of many presentations of post-Keynesian theory. I believe that it is better to present a coherent post-Keynesian view, and then contrast with neoclassical thinking only if necessary.

- There will be a chapter on yield curve modelling. This is a continuation of the work on empirical recession models, but with much more technical detail. Although this work could have been part of the present volume, the discussion of interest rate formation is tied to neoclassical economics – since central bankers are largely informed by

---

3   The *econ_platform* code is found at https://github.com/brianr747/platform. The code to generate (most) charts is found at https://github.com/brianr747/brian_books. Some examples use the *sfc_models* package.

4   This package is described in my book *An Introduction to SFC Models Using Python.* The source code is available at https://github.com/brianr747/SFC_models.

neoclassical theory.

- Housing market analysis has been deferred to the second volume, as its story is tied to interest rate policy.

- A comparison of competing explanations for recessions versus history for a group of developed countries.

- A longer discussion of my argument of why I believe that recessions cannot easily be forecast, and what that means for economic theory.

One thing to note about the deferred topics is that they will be far more demanding from a reading perspective. I have little choice but to discuss some quite advanced mathematics, as that is the preferred idiom of neoclassical economists.

1.5   The Pandemic of 2020

This section was written just before the final formatting work of the text. At the time of writing, economic activity has contracted in an alarming fashion, as a result of the decisions by authorities to restrict movements to prevent the spread of the viral disease termed COVID-19.

It is somewhat interesting timing to release a book on recessions near the inception of what is projected to be the most rapid contraction of economic activity recorded in modern history. One question a casual reader might ask: did I predict this recession? The answer is that I did not do so (except perhaps too late to do anything useful about the prediction). This is not too disconcerting for me, as the thesis of my book is that recessions are inherently hard to predict using economic models.

In order to predict this downturn, one would have needed to look at the characteristics of the virus, which first showed up in large numbers in China. One could have used models of epidemics and predicted the need for severe reactions to stop the virus spread. However, that forecast required medical knowledge, and an ability to cut through the fog of the reports from China. Some people did accomplish this feat. However, they had to rely on alternative sources of information; one could not have trawled through a database of standard economic time series to predict this outcome. (It would have been possible to look at Chinese data and react more quickly than many other investors or governments, but the lead time was so short that it does not meet the criteria for recession predictions that I have in mind in my discussions.)

This text lists a wide variety of triggers for recessions. Other than a few parenthetical comments added a month or so ago, there was no discussion of the economic risks created by a pandemic. From a narrative point of view, this appears to be justified. I believe that the pandemic lockdown is one of the few cases where neoclassical Real Business Cycle models appear to be somewhat plausible. The discussion of those models is deferred to Volume II, and so it would be most natural to discuss the topic there.

Nevertheless, only the recession trigger seems unusual. In my view, most of the economic difficulties are easily understood from the post-Keynesian perspective discussed in this volume. The closure of businesses obviously cut income flows within the economy. Loss of income flows leads to financial stress and failures, leading to a liquidation cycle.

Rather than hold off publication of this volume, I will add a discussion of the current recession to next volume and examine how it fits in with competing theories.

Most of the sections in this volume were written in 2019, and a good portion of those were written in the first half of the year. Figures typically cut off in 2019, as was discussion of the current situation. There was a recession scare in the middle of the 2019, with models based on the yield curve predicting recession. It appeared that those recession predictions would be incorrect in late 2019, when my initial draft was wrapped up, as activity was starting to tick up. Rather than risk mangling my text with a hasty re-write, I have left my assessment of the situation as stood in late 2019. To what extent my cautious statements look silly in retrospect, they offer an example of how quickly events can catch up to commentators.

There is already a debate whether the global economy was headed to recession (as signaled by the yield curve), and that the pandemic shutdowns just magnified the effects. This is slightly reminiscent of the situation in the United States in the Financial Crisis: the official recession dating starts on December 2007, yet there was still a debate about the arrival of the recession that lasted until the Lehman Brothers default in autumn 2008. I will wait for the second volume – when the full set of non-revised data are available – before confronting that debate.

Montreal, April 18, 2020.

Chapter 2 **Empirical Recession Models**

2.1 Introduction

Empirical recession models attempt to determine the odds of a recession, without being tied to any particular theory. One takes economic time series and uses them as the inputs to a mathematical model. Such analysis is also referred to as *econometric* analysis.

This approach is perhaps quite satisfying if one wants to approach the subject as if economics were a physical science. One takes data, and then sees what "natural laws" result. Although my engineering education was heavily tied to the physical sciences, I am somewhat skeptical that we can pretend to do analysis completely independent of abstract theory. For example, one could blindly grab the components of GDP, and develop a model that "predicts" recessions (based on the declining GDP definition). We need some theoretical understanding of what we are doing in order to propose a model.

Instead, we need to start with abstract theories about recessions and see what they suggest about the mechanisms. This allows us to see what economic time series are useful as inputs to the model, and gives guidance on what would be a useful model structure.

My argument is that econometric models have only limited success for forecasting recessions. It is possible to back-fit techniques that would have worked historically, but their effectiveness going forward is always unclear.

Not all models are forecasting models. Some techniques are "nowcasts": is economy falling into recession now? Although that might not seem too useful for those who are new to economic analysis, the reality is that there is normally a considerable fog over the current state of the economy. This is the result of the fact that the most reliable economic data take time to be calculated by national statistical agencies, and these data can be heavily revised.

One very interesting question is whether empirical recession models can be used to support one school of economic thought over another. Given the limited success of these models, my argument is that they are perhaps consistent with a wide range of theories; at best, we can rule out certain implausible theories.

2.2   Recessions as a Random Walk

One way of viewing recessions is that they are essentially the outcome of
the economy following a *random walk*. We can imagine that the economy
can transition to a "low growth" state, and this makes it easier for random
fluctuations in growth to result in a recession. This is often referred to as
the economy being near its "stall speed." (An aircraft that drops below its
stall speed cannot generate enough lift from its wing surfaces to overcome
gravity.) This is a plausible way of looking at empirical recession models,
but it dodges the theoretical question as to *why* the fluctuations happen.

One example of such thinking is found in this passage from the short
note "Does the Yield Curve Really Forecast Recession?" by David Andolfatto and Andrew Spewak[5]

> *Now, consider an economy that grows over time but where growth occurs un-
> evenly (i.e., the economy alternates between high- and low-growth regimes). Imag-
> ine, as well, that the economy is occasionally buffeted by negative "shocks" — ad-
> verse events that occur at unpredictable moments (an oil price spike, a stock market
> collapse, etc.). In such an economy, recession is more likely to occur when a negative
> shock of a given size occurs in a low-growth state as opposed to a high-growth state.*
>
> *Next, suppose that an inverted yield curve forecasts a deceleration in
> growth. Then the deceleration will entail moving from a higher-growth
> state to a lower-growth state. Suppose this lower-growth state is near zero.
> In this state, growth is now more likely to turn negative in the event of
> a shock. In this way, an inverted yield curve does not forecast recession; in-
> stead, it forecasts the economic conditions that make recession more likely.*

(This view of growth is related to the concept of Markov switching models, which will be returned to in Section 2.3. As will be discussed, the "low
growth regime" that was diagnosed by the econometric methods in J.D.
Hamilton's original Markov switching model paper was associated with
negative growth, not low growth. That is, if we attempted to identify a
high growth/low growth regime model using statistical tests, we are only
going to pick out the recessions. In order to fit a "stall speed" version of
a Markov model to data, we might need to use a Markov model with three

5   Note published on 2019-11-30. https://research.stlouisfed.org/
publications/economic-synopses/2018/11/30/does-the-yield-curve-
really-forecast-recession

states – high growth, low growth, and recession.)

We will put that technical issue aside and examine a simulation of such a two-speed growth model that generates simulated GDP growth.

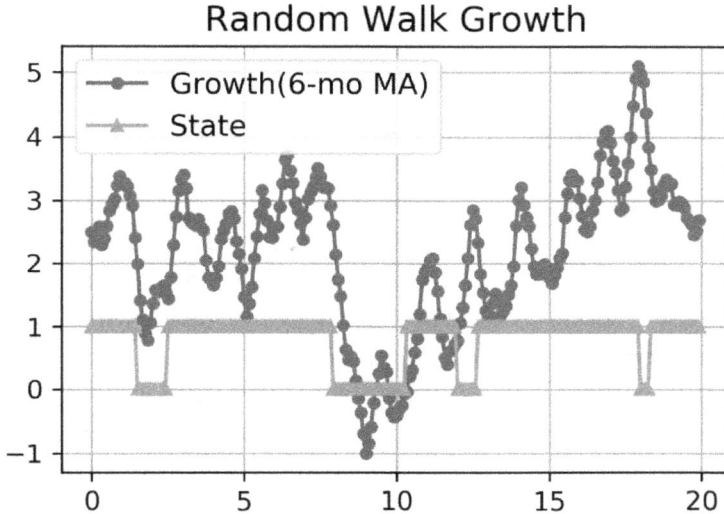

Simulated random walk growth

The figure above was generated by a Python script.[6] The line marked with circles is the 6-month moving average of a hypothetical monthly annualised rate of GDP growth; the time axis is measured in years. The non-smoothed monthly series is a discrete-time random series, and is quite noisy, explaining why it is averaged. The line marked with triangles is a not-directly-measurable state variable, which transitions between a high-growth level (1) and a low-growth level (0). The mean-reverting growth level for the high-growth state is 2.5%, while the low-growth state reverts to 0.75%. (The technical details are available in the notes at the end of this section.)

We can see that there was a transition to a low-growth state at about 1.5 years into the simulation, which lasted for about a year. Although (smoothed) growth did drop to around 1%, it stayed above zero. This is an example of an economy dropping to "stall speed," yet avoiding recession.

Just before year 8, the state dropped to the low-growth regime, and

6   https://github.com/brianr747/SimplePricers/blob/master/examples/recession_random_walk.py

stayed there longer. The result was a double-dip recession during years 9 and 10. (There were two other state transitions, but growth rates were sufficiently high that they were not visible in the growth rate.)

No attempt was made to calibrate the parameters of the model, and the underlying model is presumably too simple to capture the typical statistical properties of recessions. Instead, the objective was to generate a plot that looks similar to observed GDP data while using mathematics that is relatively easy to understand. (Some knowledge of introductory probability is required.)

What is interesting about models like this one is how they fit in with economic theory. From an empirical perspective, it seems entirely plausible that we could align such a regime-change model with various indicators (as per the discussion by Andolfatto and Spewak). If we are lucky, we might be able to get a match between predicted recession probabilities and actual outcomes. One might hope that the recession probability forecasts would be as successful as modern weather forecasters are with their rain probability forecasts.

Although I am not convinced that such a model exists, it is not the sort of model I envisage when I argue that economic models have inherent difficulties in forecasting recessions. The difference is that the hypothetical forecasting model is purely statistical and cannot answer *why* outcomes are happening. Even if we identify a low-growth state, we do not know why the economy is in a low-growth state. Furthermore, the model is vulnerable to changing circumstances. Unlike rain, governments can do something about recession forecasts: loosen fiscal policy or "relax" monetary policy[7].

(There is also the technical issue of model validation. What happens if the model suggests a monthly recession probability that is normally near 0% but rises to 20-30% during slowdowns? We would need a very long run of data to tell whether the higher probability estimates are in some sense reliable, given that realised recessions are often a decade apart in the developed economies.)

Furthermore, a "random shock" explanation suggests that there should be no other empirical regularities about recessions (other than a higher

---

7   Many adherents of Modern Monetary Theory disagree with conventional views about the effects of interest rate policy. I am agnostic on that debate, but use the conventional wording in deference to the reality that the MMTers are outnumbered.

probability of transitioning to a low-growth regime ahead of recession). This ignores such factors as debt buildups, coincidence with financial crises, etc. I recognise that some recessions might be best viewed as "random shocks," for example, a country dependant on agriculture could be plunged into a recession by a poor harvest. (Or, as based on events happening near the time of publication, the possibility of an epidemic.) From the point of view of economic modelling, such an event appears to be random (although agricultural or medical experts might be able to eventually forecast such events). Another possible source of "random" recessions might be those that are the result of external developments. Such events might be captured by a hypothetical comprehensive global model but would be most likely outside the scope of any model fitted to one country's data. However, an event like a global war seems hard to model in an *economic* model.

In summary, I prefer to distinguish between recessions being random and my argument that recessions are hard to forecast. My view is that the mechanisms for a recession are relatively well understood, but the timing is hard to pin down. This follows from the reality that market outcomes (particularly credit markets) drive recessions, and markets are notoriously hard to forecast on short-term horizons.

Plucking Models?

One variant of a random walk model would be a variation of a "plucking model," a term coined by Milton Friedman. The premise is that the economy skates along at a steady state (full employment) most of the time, with (possibly random) downward "plucks" to lower levels (recessions), and then returns to steady state growth rate. The physical analogy is a string attached to a board – it can be plucked away from the board, but tension will pull the string back to the board (without overshooting its final resting position). (What economic forces can stop growth rates at exactly a particular level – like a board – is somewhat unclear.)

A plucking model appears to be an advance over standard models where growth rates randomly oscillate around a fixed "natural" growth rate, since it generates the asymmetry seen in data – accelerations on both sides of a recession are greater than during an expansion. However, it still leaves open the question why the asymmetry exists and is less general than a regime-switching model.

I will defer discussion of plucking models to the second volume, as it fits better within a treatment of neoclassical thinking on recessions. This volume is focussing on post-Keynesian theory, and the plucking model has obvious defects from that perspective. Most of the post-Keynesian objections would relate to the assumption that there is a fixed growth rate in an expansion. (Post-Keynesians would cite Verdoorn's Law, which is that higher growth rates engender higher productivity growth.) Moreover, one can find outcomes that violate the rapid return to the steady state growth path, as in the Greek economy after the Financial Crisis (discussed in Section 3.4).

Technical Notes on the Model

As noted earlier, the source code is available on a GitHub repository. The program prompts the user to enter a numeric seed for the random number generator; the chart above was generated by using 0 (zero). The plot requires the installation of the *matplotlib* library.

The state variable trajectory is calculated by generating a random floating-point number between 0 and 1. If the state is in the high growth mode in the previous period, there is a 98% chance of staying in the same mode, while the probability of staying in the low growth is 96% (i.e., 2% chance of transitioning to low growth from high, and a 4% chance of going from low to high). The growth state is independent of the actual growth rate.

Once the state trajectory is calculated, the monthly growth rate is determined. In the high growth state, the trend growth is 2.5%, while the low growth trend is 0.75%. The value of growth is equal to the previous value plus a correction of 25% towards the trend, plus a random variable ("noise"). The noise is normally distributed, with a mean of zero, and a standard deviation of 0.8.

Since the monthly growth rate is quite noisy, the six-month moving average is calculated. For the first six periods, the "moving average" is the mean of the available data.

2.3   Activity-Based Recession Probability Models

There are two broad classes of models that produce recession probabilities: those that are based on activity variables, and those that use indicator variables to generate forecast information. This section discusses the former category: models that are based on activity variables, which provide a coincident recession probability. Forecasting models are obviously more interesting and attract the most research attention. However, activity-based models are more reliable, to the extent that data are not revised.

U.S. Recession Probability (Smoothed)

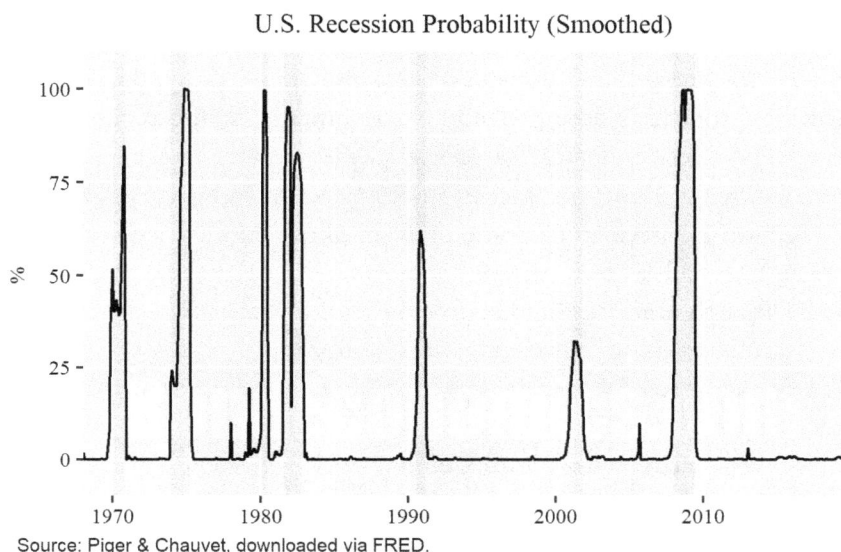

Source: Piger & Chauvet, downloaded via FRED.

Piger-Chauvet recession model probabilities

The figure above shows the (smoothed) recession probability for the United States generated by the model of Jeremy Max Piger and Marcelle Chauvet.[8] As can be seen, the probability for the last run of data (ending in August 2019) is nearly zero. This is in stark contrast to recession forecasting models that incorporate yield curves, which inverted in 2019. A simplified recession indicator is constructed in Section 2.4, and one sees that it gave a reading consistent with an increased recession risk in 2019.

Note that the end point of the series is behind the date of update (late October 2019) as a result of the publication lag of the economic data. As a result, the model is not truly coincident, but lags as a result of the publication delay. That said, one may note the absence of false recession signals in the back history, which is not a feature of the recession probability forecasting models that will be discussed in the next section.

Brief Model Description

The model is a Markov-switching model, where there is a hidden state

8   Chauvet, M. and J. Piger, "A Comparison of the Real-Time Performance of Business Cycle Dating Methods," *Journal of Business and Economic Statistics*, 2008, 26, 42-49.

variable that jumps between two regimes: high growth and low growth. In this case, the low growth regime is associated with negative growth, or a recession. If the state variable is in the expansion regime in one month, the most likely transition is to remain in the expansion regime. However, there is a low probability of jumping to the recession regime state. The recession state is less sticky than the growth state, which matches the tendency of recessions to be short-lived versus expansions.

(Section 2.2 gave an example of a simplified Markov switching model, although it had a "low growth" state instead of a recession state. This meant that the model could transition to the low growth state without a recession happening in the simulated economy.)

The expected growth rates for the following variables are driven by the hidden state.

- non-farm payroll employment
- the index of industrial production
- real personal income excluding transfer payments
- real manufacturing and trade sales

We cannot directly measure the hidden state, and so we need to infer it from observed data. We look at the divergence between the above growth rates and what is estimated by the model, and thus deduce the probability of being in either the growth or recession state. Since these variables are normally growing, the usual condition is that the probability the economy is in recession is low.

The above variables are not arbitrary; they are key variables that are used by the NBER recession-dating committee to determine business cycle turning points. An alternative interpretation of this model is that it provides a purely quantitative measure of whether the economy is in recession or not. If we follow this interpretation, it is not a question of whether the model is providing the correct recession dates, rather the question is how useful the dating procedure is. Since it historically aligned with the NBER dates that are based on a holistic analysis of economic data, we see that it is a reasonable definition.

One could choose alternative activity measures; the simplest is to use real GDP. The use of real GNP was one of the first variants of this model, as developed by J.D. Hamilton.[9] One disadvantage of GDP (GNP)

---

9   Hamilton, J. D. (1989), "A New Approach to the Economic Analy-

is that it is measured quarterly, which is somewhat imprecise given that recessions can be short-lived. However, it may be that quarterly data would need to be used in some countries with limited data availability.

One of the useful features of the Chauvet and Piger model is that it is robust with respect to data revisions. In fact, the cited paper was an analysis of the usefulness of the model when applied to data available in real time (as opposed to post-revision). My instinct is that the importance of revisions will be much greater if one attempted to fit a similar model to GDP.

Pure Econometrics

One of the beauties of this model is that it is largely independent of the macro theory wars. It is purely a summary mathematical description of economic activity, and somewhat theory-free. At most, the models may be incompatible with some potential macroeconomic models, but this would likely only happen if the model was itself completely unable to generate economic time series that resemble real world data.

Is There a Simpler Way?

The key advantage of such Markov switching models is that they provide a probability of being in recession. It may be that the user does not need such a probability, in which case, such a model may be overkill. There are two simpler alternatives.

1. Visual analysis. This is snidely referred to as "chart blogging," but the reality remains that one could very rapidly draw conclusions about the state of the economy by eyeballing the time series of the main activity variables. And to a certain extent, this is a step that is unavoidable even if you are using a formal model. You should have an idea of what is happening to the inputs of the model, and not rely blindly on the model outputs. In the worst case, there could be a typo in the model code, and the model generates a high recession probability when the activity variables are not doing anything interesting. One advantage of eyeballing charts is that one can see whether some variables are weakening, which then can lead to more careful forecasting analysis. However, eyeballing charts has a major disadvantage. As soon as there is more than one person interpreting the data, interpretations will vary wildly.

You rapidly run into the problem of "duelling chart packs" – which is why institutions like formal models in the first place. The other issue is that this visual analysis is not as useful for economists who are tasked with calling and dating recessions; they want a more formal rule for a recession call.

2. Use Principal Component Analysis (PCA) to generate a composite indicator for the chosen activity variables. This provides an aggregate variable that will rise and fall during the cycle, providing a gauge of economic momentum beyond the binary recession/expansion determination. The aggregation eliminates some of the possibilities for duelling chart packs, but it still does not offer a clear-cut recession call trigger. An example of such a PCA indicator is given in the next section.

Given that the PCA analysis provides a more general analysis tool, I would view it as being a higher priority for market economic research than a recession probability model.

Technical Limitations

One of the problems with these models is that certain model parameters are estimated based on the entire available history. This means that we should be cautious about trumpeting the in-sample performance of the model, since the model technically has access to some future information. The hope is that these model parameters will be stable over time, and so the model will not blow up as we enter new regimes.

Another technical issue is the possibility that the estimation procedure could split the high growth/low growth regimes differently. For example, if there is a secular change in growth rates, the state variable could correspond to the differing growth regimes that last decades. This was discussed in the Hamilton paper (page 372).

Concluding Remarks

Activity-based recession probability models are useful for providing a robust summary of coincident economic data. One can use them as an alternative definition for a recession. However, most market analysis revolves around forecasts, and so a coincident model may not appear too exciting (given the data publication lag).

2.4   Recession Probability Forecasting Models

This section discusses a wide class of models: models that attempt to offer a recession probability estimate, based on variables that are not just aggregate activity variables. Models with inputs that are aggregate economic variables were the subject of the previous section and can be interpreted as offering an alternative recession definition. Therefore, they are essentially coincident indicators of recessions – although they might offer a recession diagnosis earlier than "official" recession determinations are made. Instead, the models of interest here are those that use variables that are believed to have some leading information, and so can offer an inflation forecast ahead of the actual recession start.

The comments here are relatively generic. The reason is that the yield curve – technically, slopes between different tenors within the overall yield curve – is typically a dominant input to these models. As a result, any discussion of these models in practice entails a deep focus on the details of yield curve behaviour. As an ex-fixed income analyst, that is a subject of intense interest to me. The discussion of the yield curve will take an entire chapter in the second volume of this text. By deferring the discussion of the yield curve in this fashion, it is possible to give an overview of the basic structure of such models without being bogged down in a lengthy technical discussion.

Model Inputs

If we build a model that is solely based on aggregate economic activity variables, it is using the exact same series that are normally used for recession dating. So, it might have some advantages over the "official" recession-dating procedure, but it is not adding new sources of information. The models discussed here also include variables that are believed to have leading information. Some main examples include the following:
- Surveys, like those of purchasing managers.
- Financial market data, particularly the previously mentioned yield curves. Other popular choices include stock markets and credit spreads. (The stock market's mixed predictive power for recessions was best captured by the famous quote attributed to Paul Samuelson: "The stock market has predicted nine of the

past five recessions."[10])

- Credit aggregate growth (debt levels, bank balance sheets).
- Data from particular sectors that are believed to lead the economy, such as residential construction. This could possibly include economic aggregates for selected regions.
- Aggregated indicators that are based on a wide selection of series, such as a principal component analysis (PCA) output, or traditional leading indicators. These are constructed from a mix of activity/leading variables.

Putting Variables Together

The first thing to note is that we are interested in giving an assessment of recession risk. This could be done two ways: create some form of a probability model, or have an indicator that offers a forecast for aggregate real GDP growth. The second method implicitly gives a recession risk forecast, if we assume that declining real GDP translates into a recession (e.g., the two consecutive declining quarters definition of a recession). However, forecasting a recession event accurately seems in principle to be simpler than forecasting real GDP growth, so we will assume that we are working with recession probabilities.

The next technical issue is the notion of "recession probability" estimates. One could have a model that generates explicit recession probabilities, like a probit model. However, if one looks at financial market commentary, we see that practitioners use a looser definition. A typical assessment one encounters in commentary will often resemble the following: "The last $\{N\}$ times $\{a\ condition\}$ happened, a recession followed within $\{M\}$ months."

This is obviously less academic sounding than a probit model and looks less mathematically robust (what are the odds that this time is different?). However, I see little value in being too much of an academic purist about this point: we just have some non-quantifiable uncertainty to deal with, which is a factor in real world decision-making. (Keynes wrote *A Treatise on Probability*, and post-Keynesians have long discussed this issue. This mathematical controversy is a considerable detour, so I will not pursue the matter here.)

10   According to an online source, "John C. Bluedorn et al." attributed this quote to Paul Samuelson. Since I have seen that attribution multiple times, I have not validated the attribution myself. URL: https://en.wikiquote.org/wiki/Paul_Samuelson

We can generate these implicit recession probabilities by either:

- directly relating the raw series to a recession indicator variable (e.g., probit model), or
- creating an aggregate indicator, and relating some events associated with that indicator to recession events. For example, if the indicator drops below a threshold, a recession is predicted.

As for aggregation, there are a few methods. Standard choices include a principal component analysis, or the more *ad hoc* method of creating a weighted average of "normalised" variables. I will outline these in turn.

Principal Component Analysis

U.S.: Chicago Fed National Activity Index (3-month M.A.)

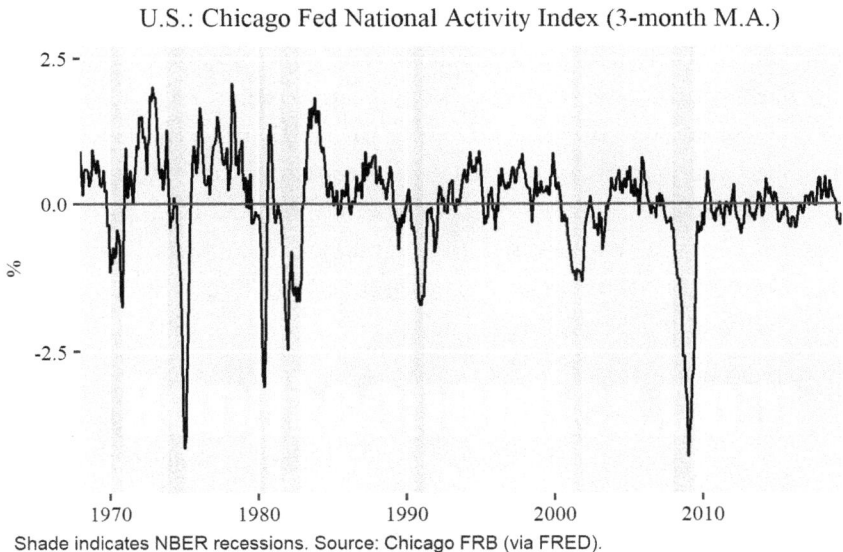

Shade indicates NBER recessions. Source: Chicago FRB (via FRED).

Chicago Fed National Activity Index

The figure above shows one of the better-known PCA models, the Chicago National Activity Index, from the Chicago Federal Reserve Bank. The 3-month average is shown, which is the usual method of presentation. As can be seen, it dips around the time of recessions. One could attempt to infer a "recession threshold" based on these historical episodes.

The mathematics behind principal component analysis is somewhat advanced. Since it is a key part of yield curve analysis, the technical description will be deferred to the discussion of the yield curve analysis, which will appear in the second volume. (I believe that the best way to introduce PCA concepts in the context of economics is to discuss its use in yield curve modelling. There is relatively straightforward linkage between the yields at different maturities, while the relationship between most economic variables is more abstract and fuzzy.)

I would caution against assuming that this mathematical sophistication should be confused for model accuracy. Principal component analysis has been increasingly popular in teaching graduate students, and my impression is that many students have come away from that training with too much confidence about the technique, and the ability to model errors. Any statistical procedure is based on an implicit mathematical model of the process generating the data, and that model can be outright incorrect. Instead, I would argue that users need to only have a rough handle on the properties of PCA solutions, and then ask themselves: what can go wrong? (The answer is: a lot.)

That said, the more rigorous PCA approaches have a practical advantage when we consider the need to transform variables. As will be discussed below, variables need to be transformed before they are input into the PCA algorithm. Following standardised procedures reduces the scope for manipulating inputs to get desired outputs. (Historically, this was known as "data mining," but the term "data mining" has shown up in modern "data science" with a different meaning.)

"Normalisation"

One common way to aggregate multiple series is to "normalise" them (or "standardise"), which is a shorthand used in market analysis that describes a two-step process.

1. We calculate the mean and the standard deviation of the time series. (The term "normalisation" appears to refer to the normal – or Gaussian – probability distribution, which is entirely described by its mean and standard deviation. However, the procedure is not really based on the assumption that probability distributions are normal. "Standardisation" is a better term as a result.)

2. For any given point in time, the value of the "normalised" series is equal to the deviation of the series from its mean, divided by its standard deviation. For example, if a series is one standard deviation above its mean, the "normalised" series has a value of 1.

We create the aggregate by adding up a weighted average of the normalised series. Since each normalised series is expressed as units of standard deviations, this step appears plausible.

I will now run through an example indicator for the United States, based on two variables. The variables are the number of employed persons (non-farm payroll employment) and the 2-/10-year Treasury slope. I have chosen these two variables for illustrative purposes only. I want to underline that the resulting indicator has various defects —which will be discussed later — and is not being held forth as a useful recession prediction tool.

I will fix my sample period to be 1977-2018, using monthly data.

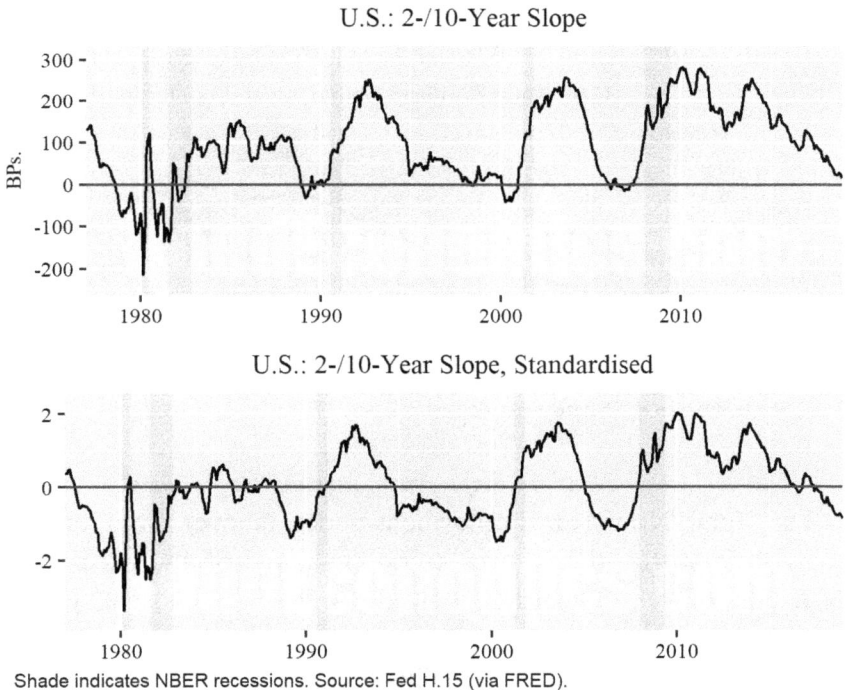

U.S.: 2-/10-Year Slope

U.S.: 2-/10-Year Slope, Standardised

Shade indicates NBER recessions. Source: Fed H.15 (via FRED).

U.S. yield curve slope, raw and standardised

The chart above shows the results for the 2-/10-year Treasury slope (based on data from the Federal Reserve H.15 report). The top panel shows the raw data, which is the slope in basis points. The bottom panel is the standardised version: the slope minus its period mean (95.4 basis points), divided by its standard deviation (91.8 basis points). (Note that the shape of the time series is unchanged; what has changed is the scaling and the level relative to the zero line.) As can be seen, the slope near the end of the in-sample period converged to zero, which is roughly one standard deviation below its average.

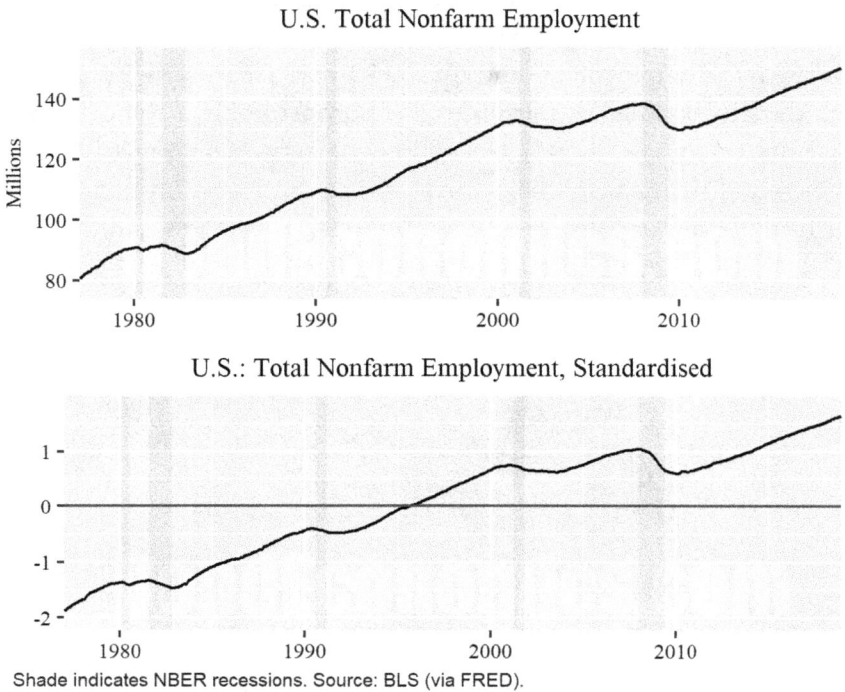

U.S. Total Nonfarm Employment

U.S.: Total Nonfarm Employment, Standardised

Shade indicates NBER recessions. Source: BLS (via FRED).

U.S. Nonfarm Employment, raw and standardised

The Total Nonfarm Employment series (above) from the Bureau of Labor Statistics (BLS) gives a good example of the need for transformation of series (which is why the series was chosen). Unlike the 2-/10-year slope, the total number of people employed rises in a trending fashion over time. We see dips around recessions, but the standardised series has a trend rise like the underlying series. The information conveyed around recessions is the temporary reversal of the trend.

We can capture the reversal in several ways. The most familiar would be to express the growth rate as a percentage change. The problem is that if we take a short period to express the change – for example, the percentage change each month – the resulting series is typically noisy (not shown). If we take the change versus the year before, we are susceptible to "base effects": if there was a large change a year ago, the dramatic change in the base causes jumps even when the current month shows little change. A more robust version is the deviation from the 12-month moving average (often referred to as "the deviation from trend." (A base effect exists, but it is much reduced relative to just comparing two points twelve months apart.)

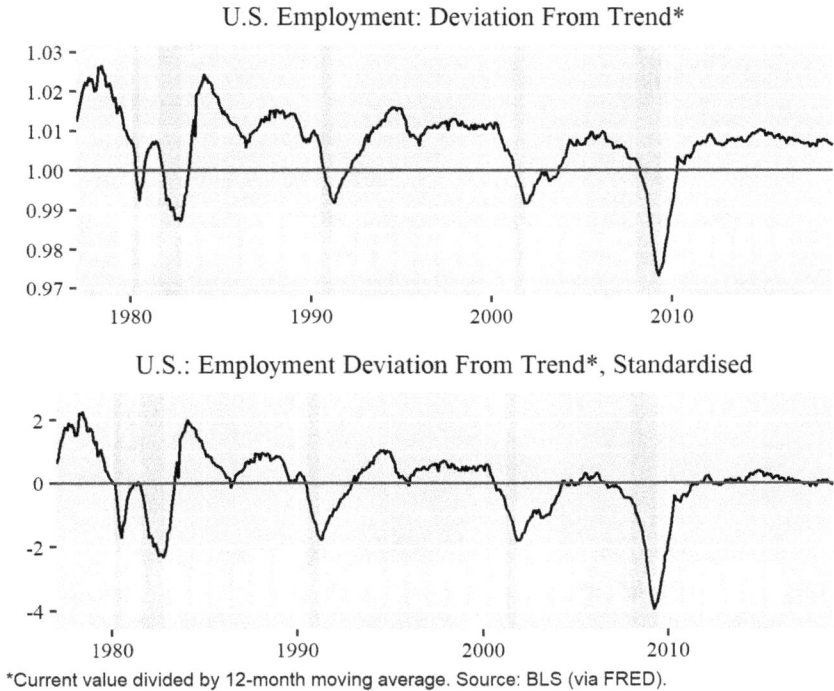

U.S. Employment: Deviation From Trend*

U.S.: Employment Deviation From Trend*, Standardised

*Current value divided by 12-month moving average. Source: BLS (via FRED).

U.S. Employment deviation from trend

As shown above, this transformed series now behaves in a similar fashion as the yield curve or the Chicago Fed National Activity Index: there is no trend to rise or fall over time. A value of 1.01 means that the current level is 1% above its 12-month moving average. As can be seen, the deviation from trend is smooth (like the underlying series), unlike a jerkier percentage change series.

U.S.: Two Standardised Indicators

U.S.: Combined Indicator

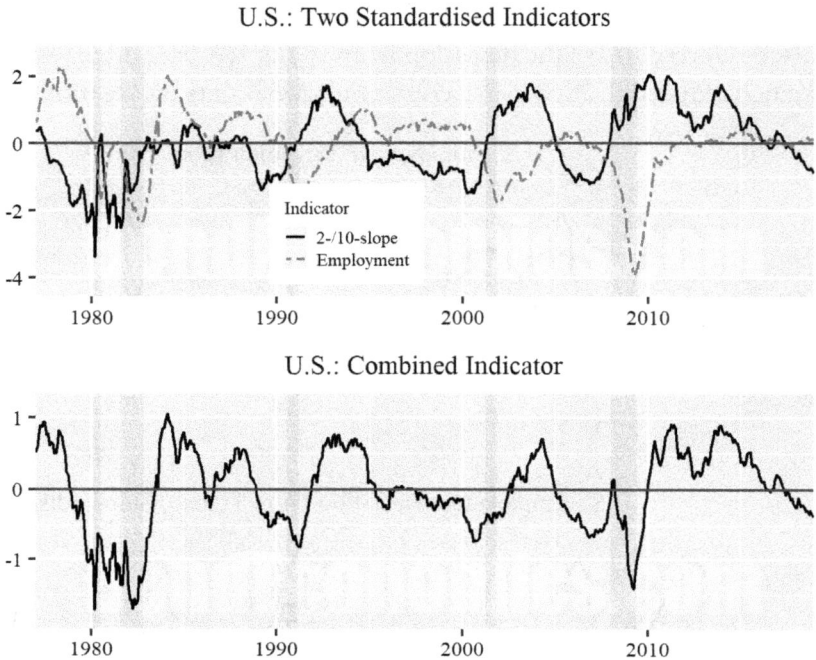

Author calculations. Sources: Fed, BLS (downloaded via FRED).

Creation of indicator from standardised component series

The chart above shows the combined indicator. The top panel shows the two standardised series separately, the bottom shows the average of the two. As can be seen, the yield curve tends to lead the employment series, and so combining in this fashion is perhaps not the most sensible option. However, they illustrate the issues around series transformation – we can just take the yield curve directly, while we had to transform the employment series.

One may note that the yield curve flattening in 2019 led to the indicator dropping to a negative level, consistent with a raised recession probability. This is consistent with other models that put weight on the yield curve. This contrasts with the activity-based indicator shown in the previous section, which showed almost no probability of a recession in 2019.

Until the pandemic struck, it appeared quite possible that the economy would avoid recession, and that the yield curve gave a "false positive." However, it seems almost certain that a recession will be declared in 2020. It is an open debate whether there would have been a recession in the absence of the pandemic. Volume II will pursue the debate about the effectiveness of recession prediction models.

Causality

One important consideration for indicator construction is the notion of causality (using systems engineering terminology). A *non-causal model* is a model where the output depends upon the future values of inputs. In the absence of access to a time machine, such a model cannot be directly implemented in the real world. In practice, a non-causal model output is "revised" as new data points are added to input series. The result is that we cannot use the latest values of the series to judge the quality of previous "predictions" of the model.

The use of non-causal model might be acceptable for the analysis of a historical episode, or an earlier economic regime (such as various Gold Standard periods). Since new data will not arrive, there will be no revisions.

U.S.: 10-Year Treasury Yield

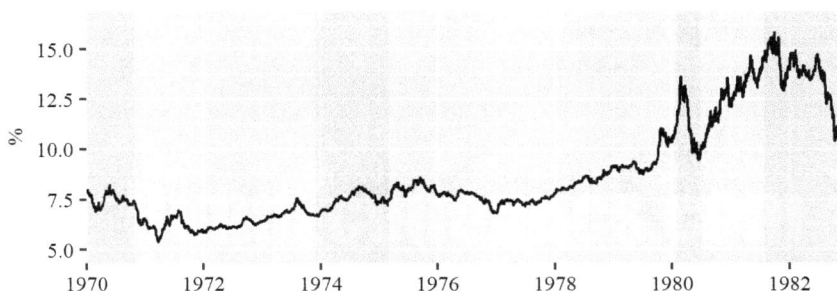

U.S. 10-Year Treasury Yield, Standardised

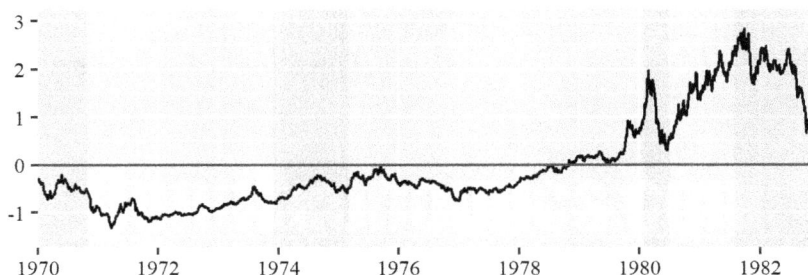

Author calculations. Sources: Fed H.15 (downloaded via FRED).

U.S. Treasury yield in the 1970s

For the indicator model presented earlier, the issue of causality arises as it used the entire period to calculate the mean and standard deviation. This was done to simplify the explanation, but it is effectively cheating: we use future information to calculate the standardised variable. The short-cut was left in place since the mean and standard deviation were relatively stable over time, so it was not cheating too much.

We can find cases where causality matters much more. The previous figure shows what happens when we standardise the 10-year Treasury yield over the period 1970-1982. As is well known, bonds suffered a secular bear market during this period (yield rising). The standardised variable shows the yield trading about one standard deviation below its mean in the early 1970s, which would be interpreted as being quite expensive. However, this expensive valuation is dependent upon us knowing the average yield for all of 1970-1982: which means we would have needed to have forecast the future path of interest rates to know that they were below average.

In order to create indicators that could be used in real time, we need to use more complicated calculations, where the output of each time period solely depends on data available at that time period. Such calculations are somewhat non-standard, and so terminology used varies. In the case of standardisation, the usual technique is to either calculate the mean and standard deviation over a moving window (e.g., the moving average), or a "stretching window" that starts at the beginning of the analysis period and extends to the latest data point. These are not difficult to implement (and may be built into time series analysis packages), but the calculations are harder to describe. This is because the "mean" and "standard deviation" used in the calculation of the standardised variables changes over time. Since this calculation is harder to summarise in text, I used the non-causal calculations in describing the model (with a single standard deviation and mean).

Inherent Limitations

The rest of this section will focus on the limitations of such models. The reason for discussing limitations rather than the advantages of such models is based on my assessment of how users perceive them. People are attracted to mathematical models, and the more complex, the better. The problem is that the mathematical complexity, as well as the attractions of using "cutting edge" econometric research[11], distracts us from the underlying structure of the model.

11   For an investment firm or similar, being able to claim that one is using "state-of-the-art" mathematical models is a huge competitive ad-

Training Against Isolated Data Points

One structural issue we face with such models is that they are attempting to match a binary variable – the status of the economy being either in or out of recession. In the early post-World War II decades, recessions were more frequent, and so there are a lot of episodes to fit our indicators against. However, since 1990, recessions have hit the United States roughly once per decade. (The situation is harder for modellers in Australia, which has largely managed to avoid recession in recent decades.) If we accept that there may be structural changes in the economy that lead to the choice of indicator variables changing, we are searching data sets for events that happened only a few times. The obvious risk is that we end up searching for an exact repeat of a few recession episodes.

The next issue is that we are sensitive to the methodology used for recession dating. In the United States, I would argue that one theme of the literature is that the NBER recession dates are robust to changes to the methodology of the analysis of activity variables (so far). When we start to look at other countries, we may find that recession dating is more controversial, which obviously casts questions on the validity of models trained on a particular data set.

For the post-1990 period, we also need to be concerned about the nature of recessions. For the United States at least, recessions coincided with some form of a financial crisis. Although I believe that there are good theoretical reasons for financial crises to cause recessions, we only need to look at the early post-World War II period to see examples of recessions that happened independent of financial crises. As was observed by Minsky at the time, the post-war financial system was exceedingly robust, as a result of a strong regulatory regime and a cautious private sector (animal spirits were dampened by the memory of the Great Depression). One might hope that regulators and credit investors learned something from the Financial Crisis, and so it is entirely possible that we can have a recession without large financial entities blowing themselves up.

Finally, there is the issue of small dips in activity – technical recessions. If there is such a dip, we need to ask whether a signal provided by

vantage in marketing materials. As a result, anything new coming out of academia is hoovered up without a great deal of dissent. That said, it is unclear how much weight the more cynical practitioners put on such models.

an indicator is really a false positive, even if the NBER (or similar body) does not call it a recession? For an example of this possibility, see the discussion of the Canadian economy around the year 2000 in Section 1.2. As a reminder, there was a slowdown of the technology sector that did cause unemployment to rise and growth to slow, yet the slowdown was not broad-based enough for the C.D. Howe business cycle committee to view it as a recession (on a retrospective basis, since the committee was not in existence at the time). This is an inherent problem with trying to match binary signals. By contrast, a model that predicts growth rates should be able to distinguish a dip from a full-fledged recession.

Economic Structural Changes

U.S.: Manufacturing Share Of Total Nonfarm Employment

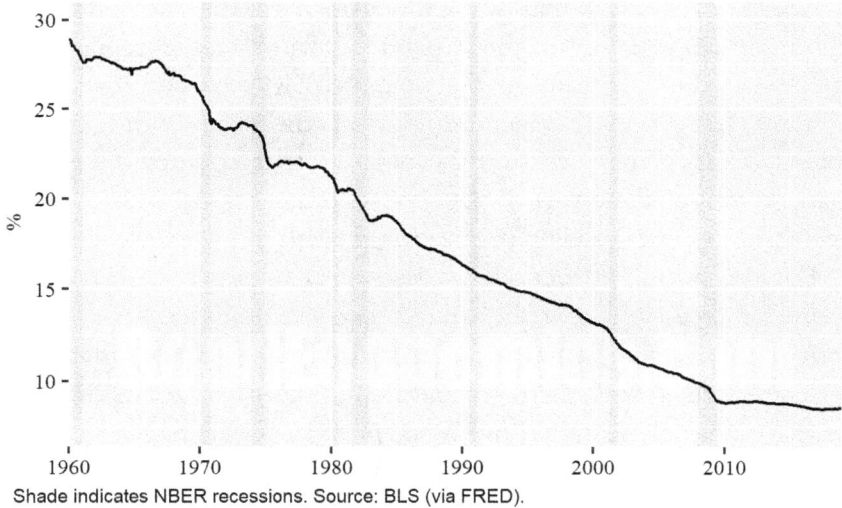

Shade indicates NBER recessions. Source: BLS (via FRED).

U.S. manufacturing share of employment

If we attempt to train our model against a long run of data, we will be covering differing economic regimes. This is not an issue for activity-based model, since recessions are defined by declines in the same set of economic activity variables (employment, etc.). For the United States, the secular decline in the manufacturing sector has meant that previously important manufacturing variables are less useful indicators for aggregate activity. Since there are fewer manufacturing workers as a percentage of the total, the same percentage decline in manufacturing employment has a correspondingly smaller effect on aggregate employment.

Regional Disparity

Differing regions of a country can have quite different economic outcomes, as well as different sectors. For example, we can track provincial GDP in Canada. It is entirely possible that some provinces are in recession, while others are still expanding. Whether aggregate Canadian activity will decline is just a question of the weights of the provinces in the aggregate. This case is examined in more detail in Section 3.3.

This means that indicators related to a particular industry may correctly call a regional recession but miss on aggregate activity. Once again, we need to ask whether this is truly a false positive.

Financial Market Shenanigans

Many of these forecast models are highly reliant on inputs that are financial market variables. The correct way to interpret them is that the model is giving a probability of recession that is priced into markets – under the strong assumption that market behaviour matches historical patterns.

If one is involved in financial markets, one needs to be mindful of circular logic. So long as we accept the assumption that behaviour matches previous norms, we should trade the markets involved using the indicator only if our personal view on recession odds differs from what is implied by the markets. The alternative is that as we end up trend following we put on curve flatteners because the model says that there is a high probability of recession – but that probability is based on the previous flattening of the curve. One ends up following past trends – which works, until it doesn't.

Since I will be discussing the yield curve at length in Volume II, I will briefly comment on some other financial market indicators that are used.

- **Credit Markets.** Various credit spreads – particularly bank-based spreads – are popular indicators. The question is whether we are extrapolating the experience of recent recessions forward (as noted earlier). It is entirely possible that the investment grade credit markets (which these indicators are usually based on) can sidestep a recession. For example, large banks have a great many mechanisms to manage the credit losses that they will expect from their small customers, up to and including bailouts from the central bank. (The branch banking model of the United States has the tendency that any downturn will wipe out some small regional banks.) It takes quite a bit of incompetence to put a large bank into bankruptcy.

- **Equity Markets.** Equity markets are supposed to be discounting an infinite stream of cash flows, not the next few months of activity. Theoretically, the effect of a recession on stock prices should be small. That said, equity markets do tend to fall ahead of recessions. This makes sense if we believe that equity market pricing is closer to extrapolating the last few data points out to infinity. However, equity markets are volatile, and so periods of falling prices are expected to happen periodically. As a result, we should expect some false positives: stock prices falling in the absence of recession. Finally, large equity indices are dominated by multinationals; it is unclear how much their prospects are tied to the domestic economy of where they are listed. For example, a country could avoid a downturn while the other major economies are in recession, and it is likely that its domestic equity indices will still fall in tandem with those of its overseas peers.

- **Commodities.** One of the interesting regularities of U.S. recessions is that they tended to be preceded by oil price spikes. (Discussed in Section 5.4 of *Interest Rate Cycles: An Introduction,* and in Section 4.7 in this volume.) There might be other examples one could find. The basic problem with using commodity prices as an indicator is the markets are global. It is possible that a country's cycle will be independent of the global cycle. Furthermore, China has been a major source of commodity demand, while its domestic economy is somewhat isolated from the rest of the world (if we dis-aggregate its export industries from the rest of the domestic economy). That said, for some commodity producers, commodity prices may be all we need to forecast recessions. The nominal income loss from a price fall may be enough to swamp any other factors in the economy.

Summary

Financial market participants and forecasters are very interested in developing models that predict recession probabilities. In some cases, the development of similar models is part of their job description. As a result, this is an ever-growing body of research, and the reader is encouraged to search for the latest developments. Even if one is not as skeptical as the author about the potential of these models, one needs to keep in mind the generic weaknesses of these models. The structural defect of academic research is that papers need to make strong claims of usefulness in order to be published, and so the discussion of weaknesses is necessarily minimised. (These tend to be observed in later research that is positioning itself as an advance past the earlier work.)

2.5   Unemployment Rate-Based Recession Indicators

A special case of activity-based recession forecasting models is those that use only the unemployment rate. This is of interest since it is associated with some recent research by Claudia Sahm. In Sahm's work, she showed that the unemployment rate itself is a good indicator of NBER-defined recessions in the United States. My view is that this rule is useful (under current institutional arrangements) as we could use it (or a similar rule) to define what a recession is.

Sahm's Trigger Rule

In "Direct Stimulus Payments to Individuals," Claudia Sahm[12] discusses the use of direct payments to individuals as a way of counteracting recessions; a policy I would describe as an "active automatic" stabiliser (as opposed to the usual passive automatic stabilisers, like unemployment insurance or a Job Guarantee).This policy stance has been referred to as "the Sahm Rule." I will discuss the fiscal policy aspects of this in Section 3.5. In this section, I will discuss the rule for the determination of recessions, which could be described as the "Sahm Trigger Rule."

The rule is straightforward: the 3-month average of the (U-3) unemployment rate needs to rise by at least 0.5% versus its minimum values over the previous 12 months, not including the current month. If one wanted to have the clean-looking floor at zero while replicating Sahm's numerical results, just compare the 3-month average to the minimum over the past 13 months, including the current month.

---

12   "Direct Stimulus Payments to Individuals," Claudia Sahm, pages 67-92 of *Recession Ready: Fiscal Policies to Stabilize the American Economy*, Brookings Institute, 2019. Sahm's chapter is available at: https://www.brookings.edu/wp-content/uploads/2019/05/ES_THP_Sahm_web_20190506.pdf

Sahm Trigger Rule: U.S. Unemployment Rate* And Recessions**

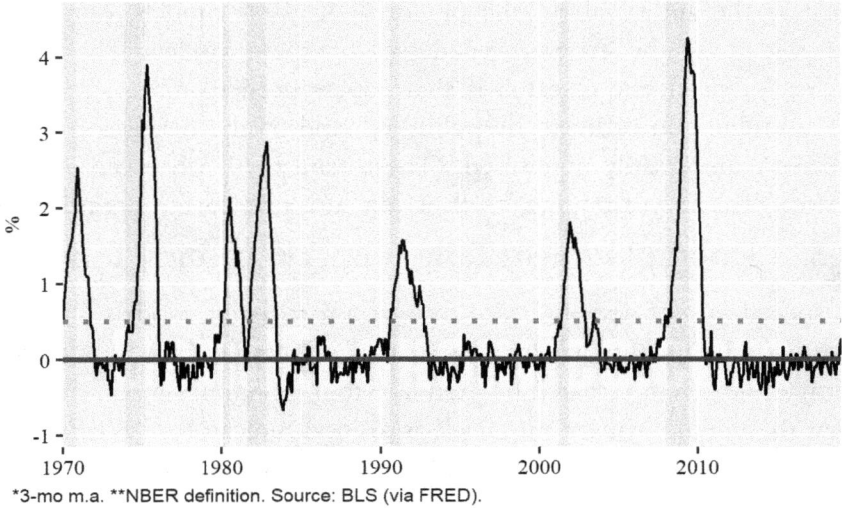

*3-mo m.a. **NBER definition. Source: BLS (via FRED).

Sahm Trigger Rule: United States

The figure above shows the results of the indicator for the interval 1970-2018 (the time frame looked at by Sahm). As can be seen, it captures the NBER-defined recessions, with no false positives.

Rule Robustness

One immediate concern would be the broader applicability of the rule. When we apply the rule to Canadian data (next figure), we see some discrepancies between it and C.D. Howe's Business Cycle Committee's recession dating decisions.

We see that the moving average of the unemployment rate did breach the 0.5 rise mark on a few occasions which were not defined as recessions by the Business Cycle Dating Committee of the C.D. Howe Institute. (These would be termed "false positives.") That said, as was noted in Section 1.2, the Bank of Canada did cut rates during recent slowdowns that were not defined as recessions. As such, one could argue that the trigger rule has some advantages over the methodology used by the C.D. Howe committee.

Sahm Trigger Rule: Canadian Unemployment Rate* And Recessions**

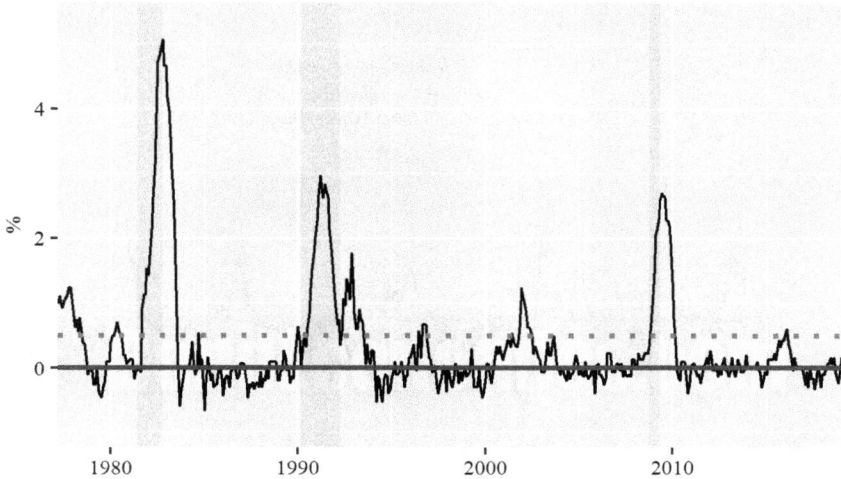

*3-mo m.a. **C.D. Howe definition. Source: Statscan.

Sahm Trigger Rule: Canada

The next angle of discussion is the construction of the rule. In my experience, some analysts place too much emphasis on the exact details of indicator construction. That is, we need to replicate the rule *exactly*, and apply the rules as specified in the original paper. Any deviation from the original result is viewed as something completely different. This perhaps reflects the culture of economics academia for defining original research. However, we need to be flexible and realise that there is an infinite number of time series filters that could be tweaked to generate almost the same recession trigger dates on the available back history. This means that there is no effective way of distinguishing these variant rules. Since we are not working with models of economic fundamentals, there is no theoretical reason to prefer one variant over the other; what matters is that they are capturing the same underlying dynamics.

U.S. Unemployment Rate Indicators

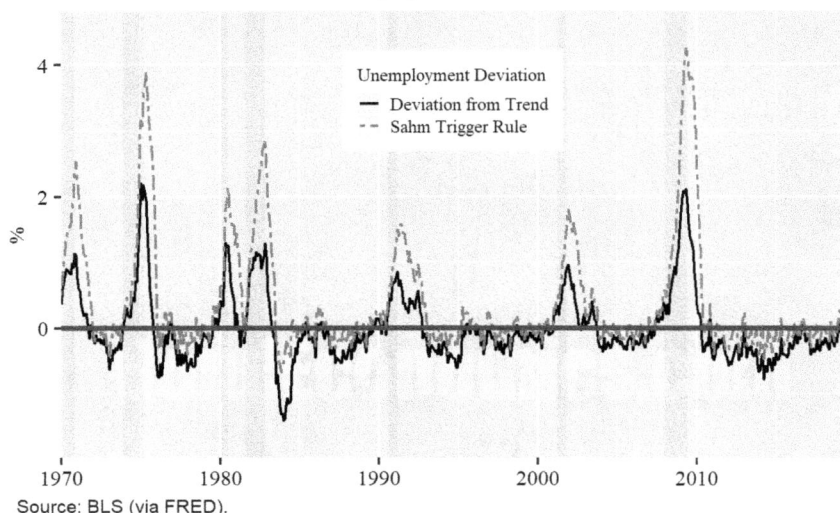

Source: BLS (via FRED).

Comparison of unemployment rate indicators

As an example, one standard alternate way to the dynamics of interest – qualitatively, a "rapid" rise in the unemployment rate – would be to look at the deviation of the unemployment rate from its trend. Mathematically, this is the difference between a time series and its moving average, typically 12 months for monthly data. The chart above compares the deviation of the unemployment rate from its 12-month moving average versus the indicator developed by Sahm. As can be seen, they are quite similar, and one could spend time developing an alternative formulation.

Although the difference does not appear to matter much when looking at back history, it affects how the indicator is used in real time. What happens when the indictors rise close to the trigger levels that were determined by analysis of the back history? For example, the deviation from trend indicator might hit its trigger level in a month, while the indicator using Sahm's construction might be short of its trigger. If we want to use a recession indicator as a binary on/off signal input to investment decisions (for example), this could easily affect performance (since returns are quite volatile around turning points). If we are back-testing the indicators, there are likely to be only a few points in time when they deviate from each other, and so the evaluation is highly dependent on one or two episodes.

In order to avoid this sensitivity to a few episodes, we need to make performance comparisons in some probabilistic fashion, which provides a smoother signal than relying on the small sample of indicator transition dates. However, a smooth evaluation means that qualitatively similar indicators – like the trigger series and the deviation from trend – will end up evaluating similarly. Although I feel that is a sensible outcome, there is a tendency for some people to demand the "best" or "optimal" indicator – which then leads to over-confidence in the indicator chosen (it's *optimal*, after all).

Unemployment Rise Triggers and Recessions

The success of this rate trigger indicator in the United States aligns with my personal bias towards such an indicator. My argument is straightforward: under current institution conditions, what matters about a recession is a rapid rise in unemployment. (I discuss institutional change issues below.) I am tempted to define a recession as a rapid rise in unemployment, and if people wish to have recession dates, use such an indicator to determine beginning and end dates for recessions. The implication is that the unemployment rate indicator would have a perfect recession calling performance (by definition).

From a theoretical perspective, one could argue that the unemployment rate has some deficiencies in this regard; we should be looking at employment growth. For example, it is theoretically possible that the unemployment rate could rise during an expansion if people who gave up on looking for jobs suddenly decided that things have improved, and they all started looking for jobs at the same time. *(In order to count as unemployed, one needs to have tried to look for work, with the exact definitions used being determined by the surveys sent to polled households by national statistical agencies.)* Although such issues will cause a certain drift in the unemployment rate during an expansion, the slow-paced nature of these attitude changes means that they are not enough to cause a rapid rise in the unemployment rate. (The evidence for the previous assertion is the fact that the recession trigger has been a reliable recession indicator historically.)

The advantage of the unemployment rate over employment measures is that they are more stable over time. The absolute size of the working age population changes over time, so we need a way to convert the number of people working to be independent of the magnitude of the net number of jobs created. This means that we effectively have to look at something like an employment ratio or divide through by the working age population – which looks the same as a ratio when the working age population changes relatively slowly (which has been the case in recent decades).[13]

U.S. Employment-To-Population Ratio And Recessions*

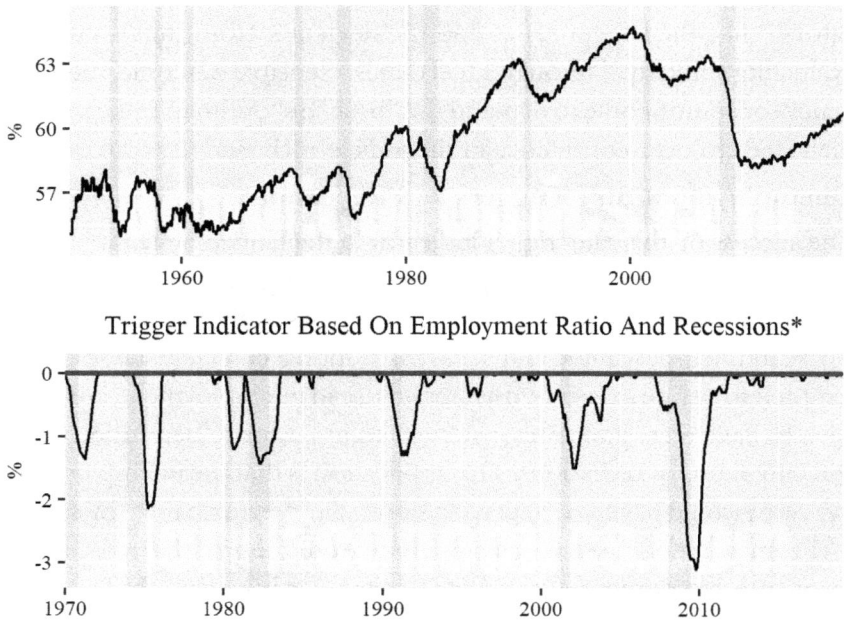

Trigger Indicator Based On Employment Ratio And Recessions*

*NBER definition. Source: BLS (via FRED).

Employment ratio based trigger indicator

The figure above shows the employment-to-population ratio for the United States. As can be seen in the top panel, there have been large drifts in the level of the ratio over the decades, related to demographic changes. The ratio rose because of the entry of women into the workforce, and over the past decade, it has supposedly been depressed by the aging of the workforce.[14] This secular drift in the ratio makes it less attractive

---

13   Markets obsess over the change in Nonfarm Payrolls in thousands, but my gut reaction is that this is partly due to the misleading precision of the figure. It easier to set up a prediction contest for the payrolls number than it is for data that are rounded to the nearest 0.1%.

14   The significance of the aging of the population as an explanation for the slow recovery of the employment-to-population ratio was a hotly debated topic in the aftermath of the Finance Crisis. The author was of the opinion that the demographic effects were greatly overstated.

for discussion (and also makes it harder to make cross-country comparisons, although one always needs to be cautious about such comparisons).

The bottom panel shows an attempt to build a trigger indicator based on the employment ratio, but with the sign flipped. (I took the maximum over 13 months including the current month, to get a nice clean upper bound at 0%.) Interestingly, the indicator does not appear to work as well as the unemployment rate-based indicator, as it has more of a lag.

Structural Change Risk

The disadvantage with just using one time series as an input to the determination of a recession is that it is vulnerable to structural changes that affect that series.

The most extreme example of a structural change would be a switch over to a Job Guarantee programme (as favoured by Modern Monetary Theory). If the programme were implemented as intended, the "unemployment rate" might be considered to be 0%, since everyone who is able to work would have *a* job that is available.[15] (Realistically, many people such as professionals would stay outside the Job Guarantee and instead search for jobs matching their skills. They would not be involuntarily unemployed, whether they would be part of the measured unemployment rate is unclear.) We might need to switch over to an indicator based on the percentage of the working force within the Job Guarantee programme; a rise in this percentage would indicate a contraction of private sector employment. Calibrating such an indicator would be difficult initially, as there would be no history to work with.

Less extreme changes could also affect the measured unemployment rate. For example, a change to the methodology could change the reported unemployment rate, which either disguises a contraction in activity, or creates a spurious rise in the unemployment. Although this event could be compensated for by users of economic indicators, it is extremely awkward for a hypothetical recession definition that is only based on the unemployment rate. This is one reason why I would not push very hard for defining recessions based solely on unemployment – even though it

15   People who are acting in a disruptive manner would be ejected from the programme under most proposals; so unless they find a private sector job (presumably unlikely), they would be unemployed. The hope is that such people would not be a large percentage of the labour force.

may be the best definition for periods with no such structural changes.

Concluding Remarks

The unemployment rate indicator proposed by Claudia Sahm looks reasonable, and probably captures exactly what we are looking for when discussing recession risks. One can modify the rule used and get qualitatively similar results, so it should not be viewed as the last word on such indicators. The other leg of Sahm's research – its use as part of a fiscal policy rule – will be discussed in Section 3.4.

2.6   Empirical Financial Crisis Models

One variant of empirical recession models are those that focus on financial risks. This field of research saw a surge in activity after the Financial Crisis. The models that I am discussing here are partial models, that is, the rest of the economy is assumed to evolve independently of the financial sector. This limitation allows for greater attention to the details of the plumbing of the financial system, at the cost of limiting recession forecasting abilities.

This limited scope of the model contrasts with macroeconomic models that incorporate a financial sector that is prone to crises, which can lead to a recession. Such models are discussed in Chapter 5, or in the second volume (for neoclassical theory). Since the financial crisis mechanism is embedded in a larger model, it is no longer theory agnostic.

Modelling Overview

The basic premise of these models is that we can use trends in lending and other data to determine the level of fragility of the financial system. If the functioning of the financial system is impaired, this would presumably lead to a recession. The reasoning behind that logic is pursued in Chapter 5. However, these models would be of no help to identify the odds of recessions that occur in the absence of a financial crisis, and the possibility exists of having a (mild) financial crisis without a recession (the experience of the United States in 1998).

The complexity of the models ranges from detailed simulations of banking system defaults (from macroprudential models) to basic graphical analysis of debt-to-income ratios that are common in financial market commentary.

My comments on the more sophisticated models are mainly based on a pair of survey papers. They cover macroprudential modelling and fore-casting models.

Macroprudential Analysis Models

The first report is "Models and tools for macroprudential analy-sis" produced by a task force for the Basel Committee on Banking Supervision,[16] from the Bank of International Settlements (BIS). The report discusses dynamic stochastic general equilibrium (DSGE) mod-els, and traditional macro stress tests. As critics have pointed out, the popular DSGE models heading into the Financial Crisis did not include a financial sector, and thus had no chance of offering much insight to the crisis. In the aftermath of the crisis, new variants of DSGE mod-els were proposed, which include banking sectors. The subject of DSGE models will be returned to in the second volume, but it is use-ful to note that some critiques of DSGE techniques are out-of-date.

The traditional stress tests described in the paper show considerable math-ematical sophistication. On page 9, typical procedures are outlined as follows.

> The first stage involves projecting the dynamic paths of key macroeconom-ic indicators (such as GDP, interest rates, and house prices) under a certain stress scenario. The projections normally use some combination of structural macroeconometric models, VAR models and vector error correction models, or some other statistical approach. In the second stage, a credit risk satellite model is estimated using either loan performance data (such as non-performing loans, loan loss provisions, or historical default rates) or micro-level data re-lated to the default risk of the household and/or corporate sector. The satellite or auxiliary model is then used to link a measure of credit risk to the vari-ables from the macroeconomic model and to map the external macroeconomic shocks to a bank's asset quality shocks. Finally, the last stage involves estimat-ing the impact of the asset quality shocks on a bank's earnings and/or capital.

In summary, econometric methods are used to generate a shock sce-nario, and then another model is run to determine expected credit losses for banks. This can be described as *conditional forecasting*: What will happen given a particular macroeconomic scenario. Conditional forecasting is an extremely useful way of approaching economic analysis, although it does not conform to what people want to hear: unconditional forecasts. How-

16   Revised article published in May 2012. URL: https://www.bis.org/publ/bcbs_wp21.pdf

ever, the difficulty of generating unconditional forecasts means that the people who are forced to produce them are the punchlines to many jokes.

Immediately after the previous quotation, the report notes one of the problems with this technique.

> *One of the main limitations of traditional stress testing is that the satellite models that are used treat the macroeconomic variables as exogenous and ignore the feedback effects from a situation of distress in the banking system to the macroeconomy.*

The implication is that we cannot use the model output to determine the expected magnitude of the recession; the feedback effects from the impairment of the financial system would increase the amplitude of the reduction of activity in the real economy. That is, if we viewed economic growth as being a form of random walk (as discussed in Section 2.2), the effect of any shocks can be amplified by the financial sector. As a result, a deeper analysis requires a full economy model. However, it is unclear how much that matters: if the prediction is that half the country's banks will end up impaired in a scenario, we can probably guess that things will end badly. The exact GDP print is somewhat of a triviality at that point.

The stress test models described in the BIS are somewhat of a diversion from recession forecasting models, but one could imagine such simulations being bolted on top of other statistical analyses to give estimated crisis odds. For example, attempt to give the odds of various shock scenarios, then see the probability of financial sector disruption beyond a certain threshold.

Predictive Methods

The next paper I would note is a survey paper from 2009: "Financial Crises and Bank Failures: a review of prediction methods," by Yulia Demyanyk and Iftekhar Hasan.[17] Demyanyk and Hasan divide predictive techniques into two groups: econometric and operations research models. The operations research models use a variety of techniques to find patterns in data without using an econometric model; the most popular technique being neural networks. Neural networks are an attempt to mimic the operations of cells in the brain mathematically. A large number of nodes are connected together, and an input signal is cascaded through the nodes. Historical data is used to find a set of connections that allows the network to identify a pattern.

17   URL: https://helda.helsinki.fi/bof/handle/123456789/7516

They argue:

> *In most of the cases reviewed, models that use operations research techniques alone or in combination with statistical methods predict failures better than statistical models alone. In fact, hybrid intelligence systems, which combine several individual techniques, have recently become very popular.*

The complexity of neural network algorithms – and their opacity – means that I am not interested in pursuing that line of enquiry. The explosion of interest in "machine learning" techniques means that anything I write about it is likely to be out of date. Although I expect that there may be interesting results, we will run into fundamental problems I will discuss later.

Financial Stress Indices

A popular alternative approach is the construction of a financial stress index. Such indices are based on a group of financial variables that offer a measure of stresses within the financial system. One might be able to associate thresholds with the probability of a financial crisis.

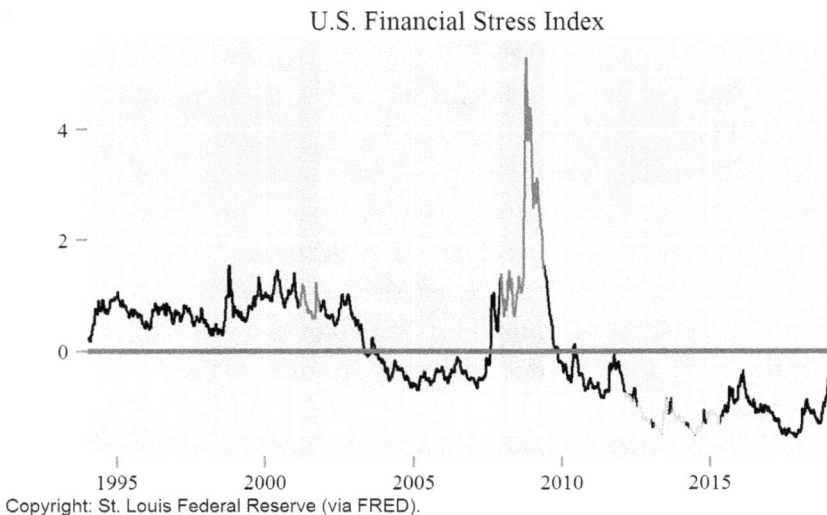

U.S. Financial Stress Index

Copyright: St. Louis Federal Reserve (via FRED).

Financial Stress Index for the United States

The figure above shows the financial stress index for the United States, as developed by the St. Louis Federal Reserve.[18] The construction follows a

18   The data are copyright by The St. Louis Federal Reserve Bank. The index is available at the FRED website with the mnemonic STLFSI,

popular convention. A number of series are standardised (the series is converted to a new series that is the number of standard deviations from the series mean, as discussed in Section 2.4). A principal component analysis (PCA) is done of the ensemble of standardised series. The financial stress index is then taken to be the first principal component.

As can be seen in the graph, the financial stress index spiked during the financial crisis, which dwarfs the previous peak that was hit during the 1998 LTCM crisis.

An alternative approach to the construction of a financial stress index is presented in the ECB working paper "Macro-Financial Vulnerabilities and Future Financial Stress: Assessing Systemic Risks and Predicting Systemic Events" by Marco Lo Duca and Tuomas A. Peltonen (2011).[19]

The components of the stress index (pages 8-9) are:

1. The spread of the 3-month interbank rate over the 3-month Government bill rate.
2. Negative quarterly equity returns (positive equity returns are disregarded).
3. The realised volatility of the main equity index.
4. The realised volatility of the nominal effective exchange rate.
5. The realised volatility of the yield on the 3-month Government bill.

Although building a composite indicator using such components is an old technique, the Lo Duca and Peltonen paper provides an interesting way of aggregating the components. The data is converted into quartiles, with 3 corresponding to the "most stressed" quartile, and 0 the "least stressed." (The signs of component variables may need to be flipped to match this scheme.) The financial stress reading is the average of these quartile indicators.

The authors observe:

> *Hollo, Kremer and Lo Duca (2010) show that the standardization method based on quartiles that we use is more robust than a standardization based on mean and variance, especially when the number of components of the index is small. More*

specifically, with the "quartile" standardization method, adding new observations to the sample produces only small revisions to the historical levels of the index (ex post stability). Large revisions of the historical levels of the index would complicate the analysis of the Financial Stress Index and its use in econometric models.

Financial stress indicators tend to be dominated by credit and funding measures, thus limiting their usefulness for fixed income practitioners. For economists or other market participants, a financial stress index offers a handy summary of what is happening in the credit markets. However, if one is attempting to price systemic risk in credit, an indicator that rises after spreads have risen is not adding a lot of value to your decision-making process.

From an economic perspective, the credit market signal should offer leading information, since the credit markets are supposed to be forward looking. That is, the initial stages of the financial crisis should be apparent in the credit markets ahead of the official recession start point. (This was true for the Financial Crisis, as evidenced by the problems with the Bear Stearns credit fund closures.[20]) Of course, this will only work if the recession is associated with a financial crisis, and/or instruments that are affected by turmoil are included.

Another issue is that some financial markets can have disjointed price action in the absence of an actual crisis. A large issuer sliding into junk status can greatly affect average bond spreads, but this would normally not qualify as a crisis – other than for investors holding those bonds. (The distribution of corporate bond spreads can be extremely uneven, even within a single credit rating tier. One possible situation is to have almost all the bonds in an investment grade index trading at a 100 basis point spread, while an issuer that is expected to be downgraded to junk status trades with a spread of about one thousand points.) Technical issues can also appear. For example, the cross-currency basis swap market has been a good indicator of problems in the wholesale markets, at least for the major currencies.[21] However, for a less liquid currency like the Canadian dollar,

---

20   For example, Bear Stearns' attempted rescue of a fund appeared in a June 23, 2007. news article, whereas the NBER recession start date was December. URL: https://www.nytimes.com/2007/06/23/business/23bond.html

21   A cross-currency basis swap can be thought of as an exchange of

the potential for a large capital markets transaction can cause a large move-ment in cross-currency basis swap spreads, even though there is no (imme-diate) risk of default.[22] As such, some pricing changes could be misleading unless the context is understood. Averaging movements across multiple instruments will reduce the chances of this happening, at the cost of slow-ing the responsiveness of the risk index.

Ad Hoc Indicators

The last type of measure is *ad hoc* analyses produced as part of market research. Common indicators to look at are debt-to-income measures. The top panel of the next figure shows one such measure – the rise in the Ca-nadian household debt-to-income ratio.

Because of the relaxation of mortgage lending standards, the debt-to-income ratio rose rapidly after 1999. This will be discussed at greater length in the second volume. However, one could look at the chart and argue that the debt-to-income ratio was at a record high pretty much at any time after 1990. This cannot be sustainable! *(As a disclaimer, I was in the camp that was alarmed by this chart after 2010, although I hedged my arguments about the implications.)*

---

matching loans in two different currencies, each paying a floating rate. At maturity, the principal values are exchanged back at the original exchange rate. One side will add an extra spread – the quoted rate of the swap – that can be either positive or negative. This spread generates the deviation from fair value ("basis") for currency forwards from the value implied by inter-est rate differentials. This wholesale market is heavily used to hedge fixed income portfolios (including bank balance sheets) and foreign currency bond issuance.

22   Another point of confusion with cross-currency basis swaps is that there is no obvious relationship between default risk and the spread. This is different than credit spreads, for which the cred-it spread is equal to the expected annualised credit loss if investors are risk neutral. (Risk neutrality means that they do not incorporate an ex-tra demanded return premium when faced with uncertain returns.)

Canada: Household Debt To Disposable Income

Canada: Household Debt Service Ratio (Interest and Principal)

Shaded bars indicate recessions (C.D. Howe). Source: Statscan.

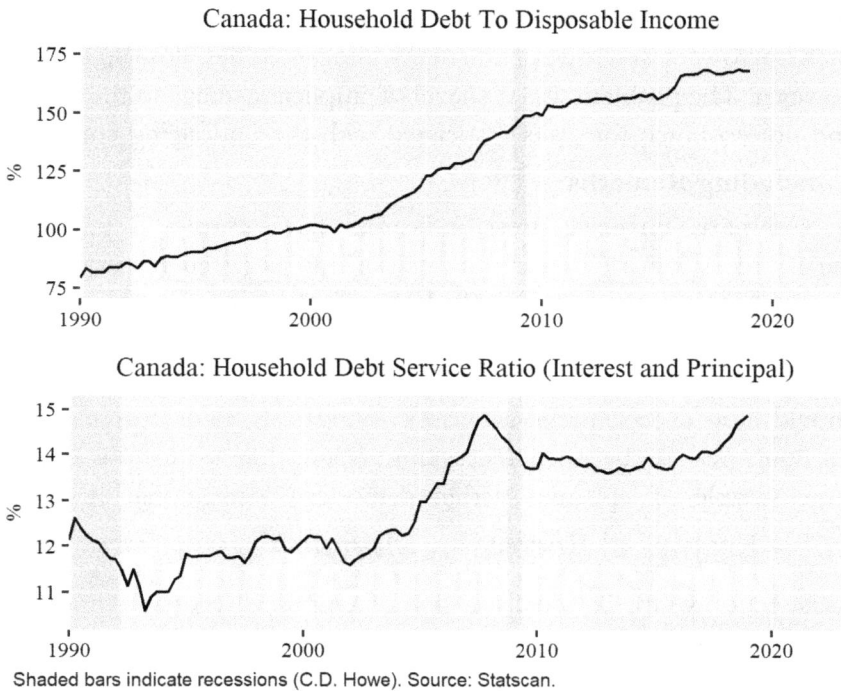

Canadian household debt and debt service

However, at the time of writing, the Canadian consumer has not imploded. Although the debt-to-income ratio was high by historical standards, it was not enough to induce a crisis. Although it looked like everyone involved took leave of their senses, Canadian households were able to keep up with their mortgage payments. This can be understood by looking at more data. The bottom panel of the figure shows the household sector's debt service ratio (percentage of disposable income that interest and principal payments represent), which rose, but in a less dramatic fashion.

This underlines one of the issues with the indicator approach – circumstances will change over time. There may be structural shifts – Canadian households were willing to dedicate far more of their disposable income meeting to debt service than they were historically. Furthermore, after a crisis, both regulators and market participants change behaviour. Problematic borrowing will shift to new instruments and feature new borrowers who default. For example, industrial borrowers in the corporate bond market were the issue in the early 2000s recession, whereas they were not as great a worry in 2008. (Highly leveraged derivatives strategies based on such borrowers were one of the many things that did blow up in the crisis, however. The problem was the level of implicit leverage in the derivatives, and not so much the risks associated with the underlying corporations.)

Concluding Remarks

In summary, financial stress indicators have a role in the monitoring of recession risk, given the relationship between recessions and financial disruptions. (This will be returned to in greater depth in Chapter 5.) However, one needs to keep in mind their limitations, particularly if the reader is a fixed income market practitioner. One should not expect previous crises' symptoms to repeat exactly, and the long periods between recessions means that we cannot build up a large sample of episodes within a modern institutional environment.

2.7   Empirical Recession Models Versus Theory

This section wraps up the discussion of empirical recession models by relating them to theory. One of the attractions of empirical recession models is that they are straight econometric analysis, and appear more "scientific" than economic theory, as theoretical models invariably have multiple weak points (regardless of the school of thought that proposed the model). By not being tied to a school of thought, they avoid the controversies that have tended to freeze progress in macroeconomics. However, empirical models have one common defect: they cannot really tell us *why* recessions happen.

My argument is that the empirical models offer less support for various theories than one might suppose. This is not following the script suggested by analogies to the physical sciences. (If economics were to follow the path of physical sciences, we should be able to find empirical laws in the data, and then back out a theory that explains those regularities.)

Activity-Based Models

Activity-based models were the subject of Section 2.3, and are more straightforward in the context of this discussion. Activity-based models can be viewed as an alternative method of designating a period as a recession.

There are only a few theoretical issues to consider with respect to such models.

- The first is that we cannot blindly grab variables from statistical databases. Some variables will just be alternative measures of the same concept, such as measuring employment via surveying employers versus households. Furthermore, other variables are linked by the definition of the variables. For example, so long as the workforce participation rate is stable, the unemployment rate and the number of people being employed move inversely to each other.[23]

- The second is that we have reason to believe that other variables will be related. For example, if we believe in the concept of a production function, output on a monthly basis should be correlated to the changes in aggregate hours worked. (This is because the capital stock does not vary appreciably on a month-to-month basis, and productivity is relatively stable over the short run.) To the extent this is true, we should expect employment and production to move together by this production relationship. (I would not expect to find such a relationship in aggregate data at present, as output in many parts of the service sector is not directly related to employment. However, it should hold for manufacturers, where production can be put into inventory.)

- The final theoretical issue is: why should recessions be particularly interesting in the first place? For example, if we believed that economic activity was the result of some steady state glide path plus random disruptions, why do we not see changes in economic variables as being akin to dice rolls? That is, one month employment goes up, then, the next month it goes down, etc. If growth were truly random, we would expect some strings

---

23   Employment is usually defined in terms of the total number of workers employed, whereas the unemployment rate is the percentage of the labour force that is not working. For example, stay-at-home spouses or students are not looking for jobs, and so are not counted as unemployed. However, the percentage of the population in the labour force is not constant, and so if it fell, it is possible for unemployment to fall without the number of workers employed changing.

of negative employment changes to be stuck together. Furthermore, different economic activity variables could be largely uncorrelated with each other, modulo the issue of variables that are naturally correlated (as previously noted).

The last point is the one that had a direct impact on discussion of theory. For example, if recessions were solely the result of random "die rolls," we could either accept or reject models based on whether they generate economic data that are random. Otherwise, properly constructed theoretical models should incorporate relationships between economic variables that exist because of the construction of the economy. As a result, a model that is an alternative definition of recession does not add enough information to reject a theoretical model.

Forecasting Models

Once we hit the much larger class of forecasting models, there is a greater tie to theory. However, even there, it is unclear how strong the conclusions are that we can draw from existing models.

One could attempt to build a forecasting model purely by ransacking a database of economic time series. In the worst case, we take 10,000 economic time series, and slap them into some equivalent of a neural net, and have a giant black box that generates recession probability signals.

The popularity of these black box approaches in academia and in industry rises and falls over time. Their popularity has risen recently, under the guise of "data science." I ran into the first generation of neural net applications in control systems back in the early 1990s when I was doing my doctorate. Neural nets made almost no headway into control systems, precisely because they are black boxes. People want to know whether their engineering systems – such as aircraft – are stable when they operate. If we are working with a black box, we cannot be sure how well the system will behave if the real-world system behaviour diverges from the theoretical models used. The application of this critique to economics is straightforward: no matter how well a black box fits historical data, if we do not really understand the mechanisms behind it, we have no way to judge whether that good fit will hold up going forward.

If we eschew black boxes that lump together inputs, we tend to see that the best inputs for forecasting models are based on variables that incorporate some form of expectations. The main classes of "expectations variables" are:

- financial market variables (e.g., yield curve slopes);
- surveys of economists;
- surveys of industrialists, such as purchasing managers.

I am relatively comfortable with the surveys of industrialists: they are supposed to be measures of what they see in activity, such as customer orders. If firms see fewer incoming sales orders, it is straightforward to see that they will themselves cut back on production. As a result, it would not be surprising that things like purchasing manager surveys mechanically lead other economic activity variables (like employment). When manufacturing was more dominant economically, purchasing manager surveys were one of the top indicators to track. However, the shift towards services means that there is less of a manufacturing inventory cycle, while it is hard to design similar surveys for services.

Once we get to surveys of economists or looking at market prices, we run into theoretical difficulties. The human beings behind these expectations-based series must get their expectations from *somewhere*. If they know something useful about the future, we should look at what they are looking at.[24]

Various theories may suggest which set of expectations are interesting. In fact, theory has presumably driven which surveys are undertaken and followed. However, different theories could easily come up with the same list of candidate expectations to track. For example, it is not hard to predict that surveys of the state of customer orders would be useful information for judging the state of the manufacturing cycle.

---

24   The rebuttal to my logic is the argument is that there is a "wisdom of crowds": large numbers of people can generate average forecasts that are far more accurate than any individual's guess. A typical example is a contest based on guessing the number of small objects in a large jar. Most participants have no idea what the correct answer is, yet the average often ends up close to the correct value. However, fixed income markets and the professional economist forecaster community represent a small club of people, given the extreme economies of scale in those industries. (Equity market trading is far more distributed, and so a "wisdom of crowds" argument seems more plausible there.) Those small clubs show very distinct patterns of groupthink and herding.

If we focus on the most successful input – yield curve slopes – we can see the theoretical problems. Almost any economic model could suggest that yield curve slopes are good indicators. All we need are the following conditions:

- The central bank normally cuts rates when a recession hits.
- Bond market pricing is mainly driven by rate expectations.[25]
- Bond market participants are not completely incompetent in forecasting recessions.

Since it is very easy for these conditions to be true, we would observe that yield curve slopes will be useful for predicting recessions regardless of what are the best economic models. Meanwhile, the above conditions are consistent with the predictions of many schools of thought. As a result, we cannot say that the success of the yield curve as a recession predictor offers any support for a particular theory.

A mainstream economist might argue that the importance of expectations variables is a point in favour of mainstream economics. I would argue that this is misplaced: just because mainstream economists stick the mathematical expectations operator into their models – and post-Keynesians generally do not – does not mean that mainstream economics has a monopoly on the concept of expectations. Post-Keynesians are very aware of the importance of sentiment in driving economic activity; however, they argue that the general equilibrium framework is flawed. The use of the mathematical expectations operator is eschewed on the straightforward argument that such models are mathematically intractable, and that probability distributions are an inadequate approximation of uncertainty.

Concluding Remarks

Empirical recession models are of obvious interest for forecasters. However, their ability to guide our choice of theory is limited, since stronger models tend to use inputs that would be suggested by different schools of thought.

---

25   I keep seeing a number of critiques that assert that bond yields are not driven by expectations. In my view, most of those criticisms are overstated. Nevertheless, all we need is that rate expectations are a major driver at the front of the curve in order for the yield curve to work as a recession indicator. None of the plausible criticisms I have seen of rate expectations seriously suggests that expectations are irrelevant for short end pricing.

Chapter 3 Fiscal Policy and Recessions

3.1   Introduction

The aftermath of the Financial Crisis underlined the importance of fiscal policy for the cycle. Austerity policies were enacted in many developed countries, slowing growth. In the euro periphery, the Greek economy contracted significantly as a result of austerity policies imposed by European institutions.

A recession caused by fiscal policy has an interesting theoretical characteristic: such a recession may be relatively straightforward to forecast. (Of course, this is not always the case. Limited governmental cutbacks might slow growth but may not be enough to trigger a recession. This was the case in several developed economies after the Financial Crisis.) Very simply, if the authorities want to cause a recession, they generally have the policy tools to achieve this aim. The events of 2020 have further underlined this principle; regulatory policy (such as closures due to public health concerns) can obviously force a contraction in economic activity.

As a result, it must be emphasised that my argument is not that it is impossible to forecast a recession at all, rather it is difficult to forecast recessions using mathematical economic models. In the case of policy-induced recessions, one needs to forecast the policy intervention. For example, will the government impose a major austerity package (or shut down activity as a result of health concerns)? To the extent these policy choices can be forecast, they are a question of *political* forecasting (or epidemic forecasting). My argument is that we cannot reliably forecast policy decisions solely using econometric models.[26]

3.2   The Multiplier

The concept of the *fiscal multiplier* can be viewed as simple, but there are many potential complexities to analysis. In this text, I keep the discussion simple (with a nod towards the complexities). There are multiple potential definitions of the fiscal multiplier, but I will use a straightforward one: it is the coefficient relating the expected change of nominal GDP based on

26   Some analysts attempt to predict election outcomes based on economic variables. Even if these efforts are successful, this is not normally enough to predict what policies elected politicians will pursue.

an assumed change in a fiscal variable. For example, if a policy change scenario is expected to raise the fiscal deficit by $100 million (relative to baseline), and the *modelled* change to nominal GDP is $150 million higher than the baseline, we could say that the multiplier is 1.5 from the deficit to GDP.

The definition deliberately uses the vague term "fiscal variable" for reasons to be discussed later.

Model SIM

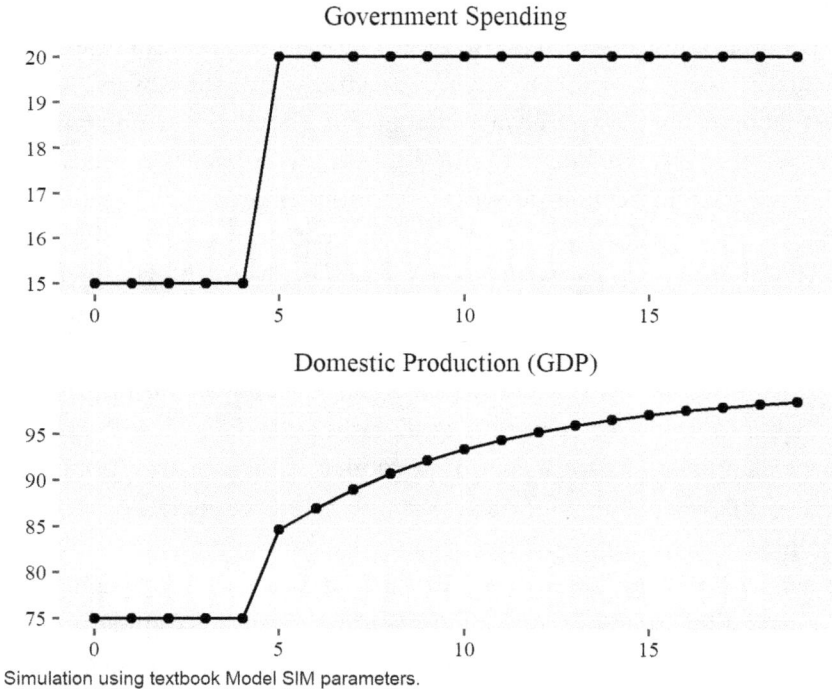

Simulation using textbook Model SIM parameters.

Government spending and production in model SIM

As an example of such a scenario, I will take the simplest possible "Keynesian" model: model SIM from Chapter 3 of the textbook *Monetary Economics* by Wynne Godley and Marc Lavoie.[27] I discussed the workings of this model in detail in my book *An Introduction to SFC Models Using Python*. The advantage of using this model is that it is eas-

---

27   *Monetary Economics: An Integrated Approach to Credit, Money Income, Production and Wealth (Second Edition)*, Wynne Godley and Marc Lavoie. Palgrave Macmillan, 2012. ISBN: 978-0-230-30184-9.

ily understood even if one is averse to mathematics. Although it has obvious shortcomings, they are easy to see and explain what they are. More advanced models have corresponding greater opacity.

The previous figure shows the results of a hypothetical fiscal expansion. The economy is in a no-growth steady state up until time point 5, when the jump in government spending occurs. Government consumption rises from 15 to 20, while GDP rises from 75 and is trending to 100. The construction of model SIM is such that the steady state GDP is a multiple of government spending – with the textbook's parameter values, the multiplier is 5.

We can also see that model GDP does not immediately jump to the final steady state, and so we immediately see a problem with discussing "the" multiplier: the effect of the change in spending properly has an effect that varies over time. We need to distinguish long-term effects from short-term effects, and this affects empirical estimates of multipliers.

What Fiscal Variable is Changing?

The fiscal multiplier is the coefficient relating the change in fiscal policy to the change in GDP, which might be viewed as a sensitivity parameter. The previous example of model SIM illustrates the conventional way of viewing it: the multiple of a spending change to the effect on GDP. For the model economy, there is a spending multiplier of 5, so we multiply the change in spending by 5 to see the effect on (steady-state) GDP.

We can view most governmental programme spending as being a dollar amount under the control of the government – e.g., the salary expenses for permanently employed bureaucrats at a government agency, or defence department acquisitions. However, the other modes of fiscal policy are not properly described in dollar amounts (although that is exactly what conventional analysis does).

- Taxes (other than poll taxes, which are nearly non-existent in modern developed economies) are specified as a tax rate structure. Changing tax rates will have a non-obvious effect on revenue. For example, an increase in income tax rates might be modelled as causing an increase in tax revenue – but that requires an assumption about what will happen to taxable income. If the tax hike causes growth to slow, incomes would be lower than projected, and so the actual amount of revenue will be lower than expected. I would argue that the correct way to look at the problem is to look at the sensitivity of projected GDP to changes in tax rates. Unfortunately, that multiplier will not be as easily interpreted as the spending multiplier in model SIM.

- Welfare state spending programme expenditures depend on the state of the economy. The number of recipients of spending is not directly under the control of the government (putting aside the ability to change eligibility requirements). The government can change programme parameters – e.g., increase the length of time unemployment insurance payments may be drawn – but the actual effect on dollar expenditures is dependent upon the number of people in the programme. We need to keep in mind the counter-cyclical nature of the spending. If everything else is equal, welfare state spending will rise if the economy shrinks. This does not mean that the multiplier on welfare state spending is negative.

The conventional way to budgetary analysis is to look at projected budgets, and work with the projected dollar amounts. One can then use a straight multiplicative multiplier to see the projected effect on growth. However, we see that this is misleading except in the case of straight changes to non-welfare state expenditures.

Further Complications

The other set of complexities with respect to a multiplier is that not all taxes and expenditures have the same effect on the economy. We can see the following effects in simple macroeconomic models that are adapted to allow for these dynamics.

- Not all private sector entities will adjust their spending in the same way for the same dollar amount of spending. For example, an increase in interest income going to a pension fund will not prompt any immediate spending in response, rather the income flow will be hoarded. Similarly, richer households appear less likely to spend out of tax cuts than poorer ones.
- Similarly, the economic effects of tax increases will depend on who and what is being taxed.
- If the government purchases goods produced externally, there will be almost no effect on gross domestic product. (The in-

crease in the trade deficit will cancel out the increased government expenditure.)

We would need a detailed macroeconomic model to capture low-level dynamics to properly model the effects of changing fiscal policy in the real world. Since such models are not particularly successful, we are stuck with approximations. This creates a great deal of fuzziness around "multiplier" estimation in practice.

My argument is that any relatively simple macro model that disaggregates the private sector will result in different fiscal policy changes having different sensitivities with respect to their effect on growth. It is only possible to generate a single multiplier in a model where we avoid any attempt at disaggregation (such as simple post-Keynesian SFC models, or neoclassical unitary representative household models without business sectors). Therefore, one should expect empirical multiplier estimation to be an extremely difficult task. As a result, I do not see much value pursuing the literature on multipliers within this text, since that will just tell us what we already can guess from first principles.

Summary

The difficulty of estimating the fiscal multiplier means that it is normally difficult to gauge the effects of fiscal policy on growth. Although I believe that fiscal policy is more important than monetary policy, much of the effect is via automatic stabiliser effects. In practice, fiscal policymakers have generally shied away from aggressive fiscal policy adjustments since the early 1990s (the euro area periphery being a key exception, as will be discussed in Section 3.4). Correspondingly, the effects of fiscal policy have often been much less visible than was expected by somewhat sensationalistic market analysis.

Nonetheless, the basic multiplier story remains pertinent for the discussion of recessions. Sufficiently tight fiscal policy will always be enough to generate a recession, and one might hope that a well-timed fiscal boost could prevent recessions (as will be returned to in Section 3.5).

3.3   Regional Recessions and Fiscal Policy

Regional economic divergences add to the complexity of recession dating. The fact that economic conditions vary across the country also complicates the policy response to recessions. An across-the-board stimulus package may be ill-advised if some regions of a country have overheating job markets as a result of certain industries bucking economic trends seen elsewhere. One of the distinctive features of Modern Monetary Theory is the emphasis on sectoral and regional divergencies (although it should be noted that individual economists in other schools of thought are well aware of these issues).

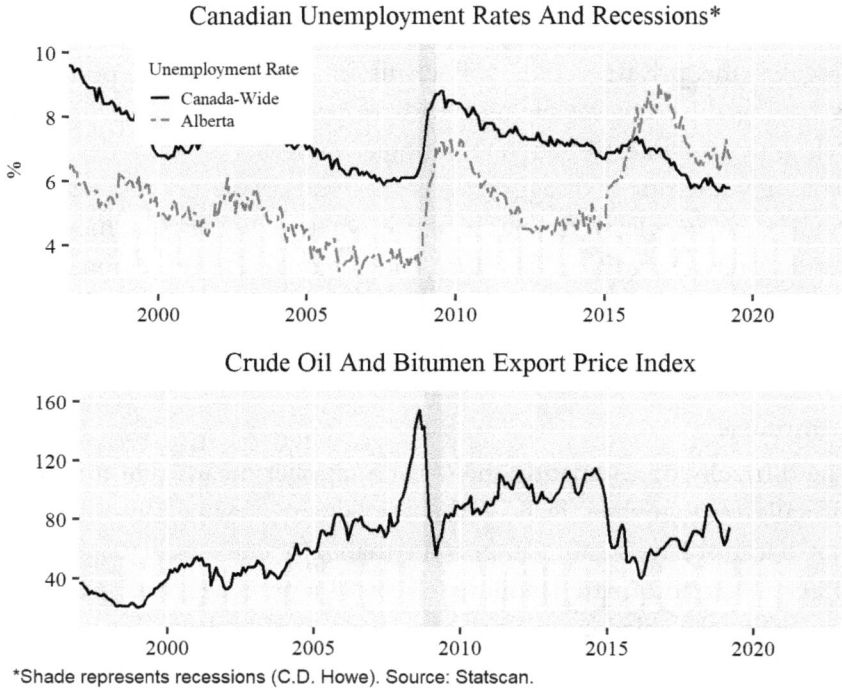

Canadian Unemployment Rates And Recessions*

Crude Oil And Bitumen Export Price Index

*Shade represents recessions (C.D. Howe). Source: Statscan.

Canadian and Albertan unemployment rates and energy prices

The figure above demonstrates a recent example of diverging fortunes within the Canadian economy. The top panel shows the unemployment rate for 15- to 64-year-old Canadians and for those living in the Province of Alberta. Until 2015, the Albertan unemployment rate moved in tandem with the Canada-wide rate, although at a lower level. However, the weakness in energy export prices after 2015 (bottom panel) hit the Albertan economy hard. (Albertan crude oil production is now dominated by the output of the tar sands, and those prices were notably weak versus globally traded oil prices since there are only limited options for exporting the products.) The rise in the Albertan unemployment rate was comparable to that of 2008 crisis. By contrast, the Canadian unemployment rate only nudged higher.

For someone based in Alberta, the fact that the national economy avoided recession could have been viewed as a piece of trivia. Business plans are still going to be disrupted by lost jobs among customers, as well slashed investment spending.

Some market analysts tend to exaggerate the importance of commodities for the Canadian economy. If an analyst correctly predicted the fall in Canadian oil export prices, they could have easily predicted a recession in the Canadian economy. They would have been correct for the situation in Alberta, but it would have been a forecast miss at the national level.

The existence of these divergences is one reason I am not particularly concerned about the details of recession-dating procedures. A national economy is the sum of regional economies. If national gross domestic product is on the verge of contraction, some regions are almost certainly undergoing economic contractions. (The only way that could be avoided is the low probability event that all regions have almost the same growth rate.) We will see the side effects of recessions in those regions that are the basis of our concern for recessions in the first place.

However, regional growth divergences may be of lesser importance when discussing financial crisis risk – putting aside the important exception of the euro zone. Generally, financial systems are largely national in scope, although the United States has a system of regional and local banks. Financial crises therefore tend to be national events, and there is an across-the-board tightening of credit conditions. (The Savings and Loan Crisis in the United States was somewhat regional in character, although multiple regions were affected.)

(The euro area is a currency peg system rather than a true integrated economy. Financial systems are national, and financial crises can be contained at the national level, as seen in various post-Financial Crisis episodes.)

Policy Implications

From a policy standpoint, regional divergences call into question the emphasis on aggregate demand management. Neoclassical theory is dominated by aggregated models, particularly those based on the notion of optimising agents. Interest rate policy is the preferred mode to deal with economic fluctuations, and interest rates are common across an entire currency bloc. To the extent that fiscal policy is accepted as a policy tool, it is thought of in terms of its effect on aggregate demand.

Only looking at aggregates fails when faced by regional divergences. The worst-case scenario is having some regions of the country contracting as a result of industrial weakness, while other regions are booming courtesy of a housing bubble. Interest rate cuts are unlikely to save a struggling industry – such as oil producers facing a collapse in the global oil price – while they will help a housing bubble inflate. (Housing markets will be discussed in greater length in the second volume.)

Automatic fiscal stabilisers in the form of welfare payments, unemployment insurance, or the proposed Job Guarantee programme are one natural response to regional divergences. When we decompose the fiscal deficit on a regional basis, it will automatically react to regional disparities. That is, weaker regions will pay less tax, and citizens that benefit from welfare state programmes will have their incomes boosted as a result of the transfers/wages. By contrast, booming regions will face an increasing tax bill as a result of higher income and spending.

Unfortunately, these automatic stabilisers are not enough by themselves to prevent recessions in an economy with after-tax wage disparities. For the automatic stabilisers to kick in, jobs must be lost in the private sector – which is coincident with the start of the recession. In other words, too late to stop the recession. (If one believed that expectations mattered greatly for economic outcomes, one might hope that might be enough to prevent recessions. The expected effect of the fiscal automatic stabilisers could prevent self-fulfilling cutbacks in private sector expenditures. Curiously, the neoclassical school – which emphasises the role of expectations in stabilising output – tends to downplay the effect of fiscal policy. For example, many benchmark neoclassical macro models did not even attempt to include the effect of automatic fiscal stabilisers. However, the fact that recessions occur despite the existence of automatic stabilisers tells us that the belief that expectation management is enough to prevent recessions is implausible.)

Clouding Recession Calls

The developed economies have drifted into a slow growth regime with economic volatility. In such a regime, there are likely to be many growth pauses with some regions dropping into contraction. Since I am discussing the big picture issues around recessions, regional divergences will not be pursued further. However, they will matter for market commentary, as well as for policy analysis.

3.4 Expansionary Austerity and Policy-Induced Recessions

Austerity policies – which typically cut government expenditures but may include tax hikes – are a politically-charged area of macroeconomics. In particular, the question of "expansionary austerity" was hotly debated in the aftermath of the Financial Crisis (and reopened again at the time of writing). In this section, I will largely side-step what was debated historically, and just cover more basic questions about austerity and recessions.

I greatly distrust the usual justifications for austerity policies; rather I argue that austerity policies are an attempt to achieve a political economy objective: shrink the size of government, and particularly, the welfare state. Currently, political divisions in the developed countries are largely related to views about the size of government, and so it is no surprise that this would work its way into discussions of fiscal policy.

Expansionary Austerity

I will use the article "Austerity in 2009-13" by Alberto Alesina, Omar Barbiero, Carlo Favero, Francesco Giavazzi and Matteo Paradisi[28] as an example of expansionary austerity arguments. In their article, they look at the post-crisis episode to defend the "expansionary austerity" thesis from critics (like myself). They lead off their conclusions with these observations.

> The conventional wisdom is first that fiscal austerity was the main culprit for the recessions experienced by many countries, especially in Europe and, second, that this round of fiscal consolidation was much more costly than the past ones. The contribution of this paper is a clarification of the first point and, if not a clear rejection, at least it raises doubts on the second.
>
> On the first point our main finding is that, as in the past, in the recent episodes there has been a very big difference between TB [tax-based] and EB [expenditure based] fiscal adjustments. The former have indeed been very costly in terms

28   "Austerity in 2009-13", by Alberto Alesina, Omar Barbiero, Carlo Favero, Francesco Giavazzi and Matteo Paradisi, *Economic Policy*, pages 385-437. July 2015.

of output losses. The latter much less so. These results are very similar to those obtained by many authors who have studied the effects of fiscal adjustments preceding the period 2010–13. Comparing our results on these recent adjustments and the ones obtained using pre-crisis data – that is up to 2007 – we did not find strong evidence against the hypothesis that fiscal multipliers – large tax multipliers and very small spending multipliers – were stable across the two sub-samples.

Our results, however, are mute on the question whether the countries we have studied did the right thing implementing fiscal austerity at the time they did, that is 2009–13 [emphasis mine].

Once we consider the final observation that they do not defend the actual policies undertaken by real-world policymakers, I am unsure whether I can disagree with the discussion in the article. Their key argument is that cutting expenditures *historically* created less of a shock to the economy than tax hikes. Although this is convenient politically for people who want to shrink the size of the state (i.e., shrinking the government appears less costly than expanding it) this could also be explained by the possibility that politicians treat tax hikes differently than expenditure cuts. (For example, I am not aware of many examples of governments focusing tax hikes on high incomes in the post-1980s era, which theoretically would be the optimal way to increase revenue with the least economic disturbance.) So long as we assume that different types of expenditures and taxes have different multipliers, such outcomes are not implausible.

This exposes the weakness of the desire for austerity policies in the first place for floating currency sovereigns. Since such governments do not face *financial* constraints, rather *real resource* constraints, we should not be analysing fiscal policy in terms of currency units (e.g., dollars), rather their effect on the real economy. The simple statistical methodology those authors use – which only looks at budget balance data – cannot hope to capture those issues.

"Success" Stories

The next chart shows a pair of key examples of expansionary austerity cited by Alesina *et al.*: Canada and Spain in the 1990s. The figure shows general government (that is, all levels of government) expenditures as a percentage of GDP, taken from the IMF *World Economic Outlook*. During the 1990s, both countries lowered their expenditures, and avoided recession during that period.[29]

29   The Canadian recession bars are from the C.D. Howe institute,

Canadian General Government Expenditures

Spanish General Government Expenditures

Source: IMF. Shade represents recessions (C.D. Howe, Spanish Econ. Assoc.).

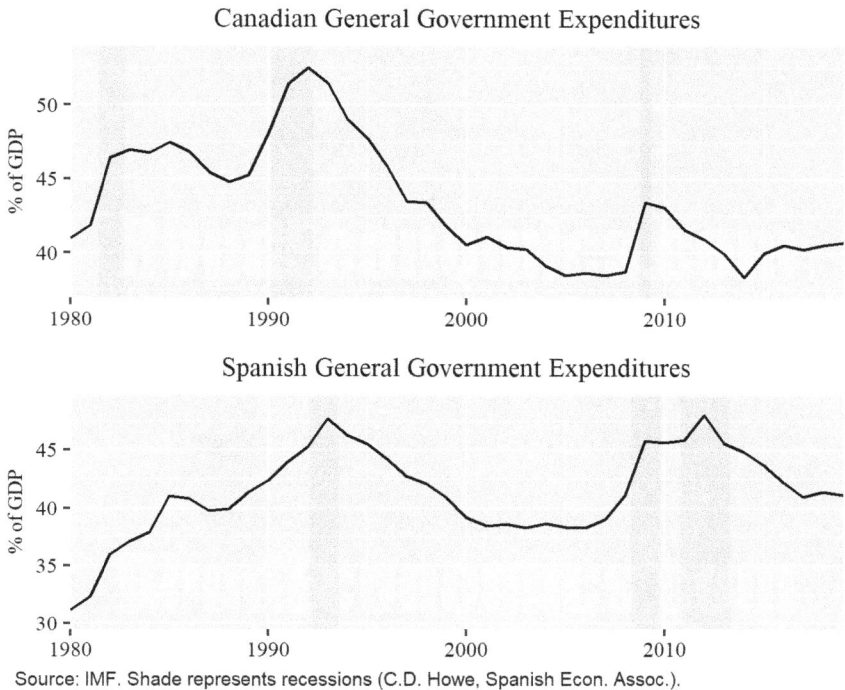

Government expenditures in Canada and Spain

However, one might note that these countries also were boosted by the external sector during this period: the weakened Canadian dollar boosted the trade balance, and Spain entered its "euro convergence boom." We should not be too surprised that an economy can absorb government expenditure cuts if the private sector is entering a boom for other reasons. In my view, these other factors are far more important than the textual analysis of policy-makers' speeches ("the 'narrative' method pioneered by Romer and Romer").

The debate about their methodology used by Alesina *et al.* is beyond the scope of this text. Nevertheless, it is clearly possible to tighten fiscal policy without triggering a recession. That said, it is unclear whether that is a trivial observation: any advanced economic model will have "automatic stabilisers" that return growth to some

previously referenced. The Spanish source is: Spanish Economic Association (2015), "CF Index of Economic Activity", Spanish Business Cycle Dating Committee. URL: http://asesec.org/CFCweb/historical-archive-of-the-spanish-business-cycle/

form of a steady state trajectory, beyond fiscal policy. These include:

- monetary policy (to the extent we believe in the effectiveness of monetary policy),
- the action of the external sector (slower consumption growth should reduce imports),
- forward-looking behaviour in the capital markets,
- the fact that expenditures are measured on a pre-tax cost basis, while taxes will "recover" some of those expenditures (e.g., government employees pay taxes on their income and often on their consumption via value-added taxes)[30],
- forced dis-saving by households who have lost employment.

Once we add up all these factors, we should expect a low multiplier on fiscal policy that attempts to push growth rates away from "steady state" growth; that does not mean that the multiplier for impulses towards steady state are similarly small.

If the fiscal tightening is gradual, it is yet another factor that affects our near-term economic forecast. We would normally expect gradual fiscal tightening in a currency sovereign, as politicians are normally concerned with self-preservation. The uncertainty about the effect of fiscal policy is likely to be less than the uncertainty about fixed investment (which is the focus of upcoming chapters). As such, the focus should normally be on the private sector.

Predictable Disaster

Nevertheless, when we move away from the idealised state of currency sovereignty, the possibility of fiscal policy-induced recessions rises. The next chart shows the policy vandalism inflicted upon the Greek economy by European policymakers. Such a decline in nominal GDP in a developed country was presumably unthinkable to the generation that declared that modern policymaking tools ushered in "The Great Moderation."

30   Imagine that the (general) government pays an employee a $1000 wage, and the average tax rate paid is 30%. This means that the net cost to the government is $700. (In places like Canada, the taxes may be collected by other levels of government, so there are effectively some inter-governmental transfers that result.) Cutting that worker's job implies only a reduction of income to the private sector of $700, which is less than the headline cut in expenditures ($1000). This reduces the measured multiplier from expenditure cuts to output.

Greek Nominal GDP

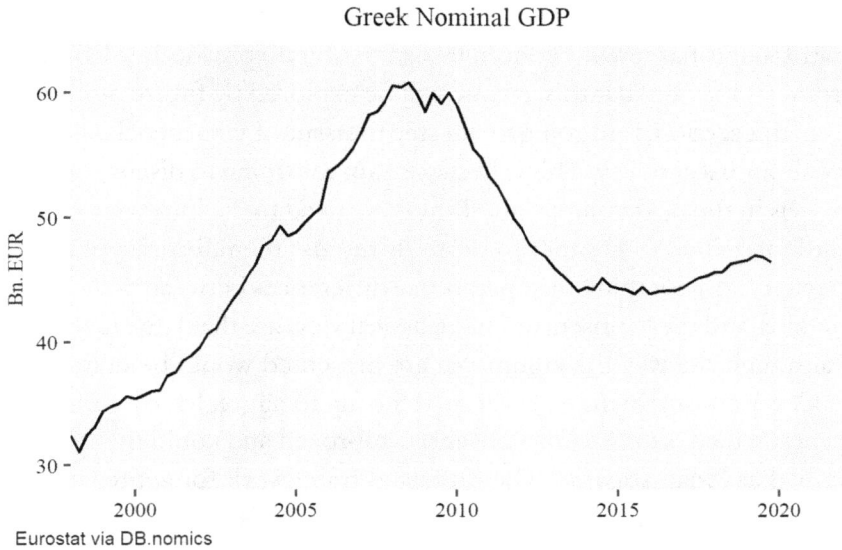

Eurostat via DB.nomics

Nominal GDP of Greece

I highlight this as this creates an exception to my argument that recessions are hard to forecast. Sufficiently stupid policy can ensure a highly predictable recession. The challenge is to identify which policies meet that criterion. One can imagine any number of disastrous outcomes that result from policy choices; austerity policies were just the flavour *du jour* in the recent past. Any study of history tells us that humans have an amazing capacity for folly. However, predicting such disasters is more a question of political analysis than economic analysis. (For example, it was much easier for European institutions to force Greece into a deep recession. It is much less plausible that such a treatment would be meted out to a powerful country like France.)

3.5 Preventing Recessions with Fiscal Policy?

The focus of this book is on recession forecasting, and not on policy responses towards recessions. However, I expect that this is a subject of interest to many of my readers, so I will offer a brief outline of some of the literature.

The recession of 2020 is not a good example for discussing the ability to avoid recessions. The authorities deliberately shut down economic activity to suppress the spread of the pandemic. There was no plausible macroeconomic wizardry that could have prevented a contraction in GDP, other than having hardened economies against viral spread ahead of the outbreak. (It may be that this avenue will be explored by future policymakers.)

In this section, I am going to sidestep the issue of what neoclassical models say about fiscal policy. This is because I am returning to discuss neoclassical models in the next volume, and I think we need to dig into their rather awkward mathematics in order to properly discuss them. From a practical perspective, I do not think the operational differences between post-Keynesian thinking and the "consensus" neoclassical view are that large in this context – although the way the arguments are presented would be quite different.

Complicating matters, I will be referring to aggregate demand management – which is arguably a consensus approach and could therefore be described as "mainstream." The preferred framework for aggregate demand management among "mainstream" economists is via the use of interest rate policy, but the sympathy for fiscal policy rises and falls. I am using "aggregate demand management" as that is the most familiar wording, but perhaps a better phrasing for what I mean is "non-targeted stimulus."

Aggregate Demand Management

The use of aggregate demand management is not purely a neoclassical view; for example, post-Keynesian authors do suggest such approaches. As an example, in the article "Fiscal Policy in a Stock-Flow Consistent Model," Wynne Godley and Marc Lavoie[31] argue that fiscal policy can achieve (in theory) all the objectives that neoclassicals claim can be achieved via monetary policy. In the paper, they propose "fiscal policy rules" that are analogous to central bank reaction functions in neoclassical models. In the paper, they note that there could be practical issues with following such rules. Interest rate policy is inherently an aggregate demand management tool, and it is largely the MMT wing of post-Keynesianism that questions the effectiveness of monetary policy. (Other post-Keynesians would dispute that monetary policy is the most effective policy lever, but in so far as I can detect a consensus, it is that monetary policy works in the conventional fashion.)

The question arises: what is aggregate demand management? It is what results when we approach the question of stabilising economic aggregates

31   This appears as Chapter 9 in *The Stock-Flow Consistent Approach: Selected Writings of Wynne Godley* (edited by Marc Lavoie, Gennaro Zezza), Palgrave Macmillan (2012). ISBN: 978-0-230-29311-3.

using models that themselves are constructed via aggregated sectors. Given the intractability of breaking up economic models into a multitude of actors (although the agent-based literature is moving in that direction), this ends up covering almost all analysis based on macroeconomic models.[32] For example, the discussion of the fiscal multiplier in Section 3.2 is an example of such an aggregated model, and aggregate demand management.

In the case of interest rate policy, the policy rate is a single rate that covers the entire currency bloc.[33] (This is an issue for the euro area, where countries with divergent economic trends is covered by the same rate, but many other countries face regional economic divergences.) The effect of the policy rate is transmitted to the entire risk-free curve, which is used to price private sector debts. As such, interest rate policy cannot target individual regions or most sectors. If we widen "monetary policy" to include quantitative credit controls, some notion of regional targeting would be available. (Currently, it is possible for central banks to target residential mortgage rates to a certain extent by intervening in the mortgage-backed securities markets. If those securities were segregated by region, regional control might be achievable. It would be more difficult to target industrial sectors under current institutional arrangements, particularly given that crafty corporate treasurers would arbitrage cross-sector funding cost differentials.[34]) How-

---

32   The "micro-foundations approach" of neoclassical models is really about aggregates, even though they might be based on a mathematical formalism based on optimising agents. Some models effectively reduce to a single agent (the "representative agent"), while others have multiple classes of agents. However, these agents are still not tied to a particular geographical location (for example), and are effectively just a way to embed extra parameters into a sectoral behavioural function.

33   At the time of writing, there are commentators discussing so-called "dual interest rate" policies, where the central bank creates a divergence between its borrowing and lending rates. I am unconvinced that this will be economically meaningful, as we will still end up with a benchmark government curve that will be used as a benchmark in wholesale funding markets. Giving selected banks access to cheaper funding is just a way for the central bank to shower profits on some selected firms, but everyone else will face a funding curve that is priced as a spread off the government curve.

34   I would like to thank other Twitter users (including Eric Lonergan

ever, quantitative credit controls have fallen out of favour, and are probably
not thought of as being part of "monetary policy" at present, even though
the central bank would have administered such controls historically.[35]

Fiscal policy can be either targeted or non-targeted, but in practice,
discretionary fiscal policy tends to lean towards non-targeted aggregate demand management.

- A broad-based personal tax cut or fiscal transfer is an attempt
  to "get money into the pockets of consumers." Since the trans-
  fer/tax cut are normally designed to hit a wide number of voters, the effects do not target areas of weakness.

- Tax cuts for business are typically aimed at measures to boost investment: accelerated depreciation allowances, etc. Once again,
  they are typically broad-based, and so, aiming at an aggregate.

- Some measures targeted industries; in the aftermath of the Financial Crisis, there were measures aimed at home renovations
  and to increase trade-ins of old cars for new ones. These measures were in a half-way zone: they hit sectors of interest, but
  were not regionally targeted.

- The main "targeted" fiscal interventions are the "automatic
  stabiliser" policies of the welfare state: unemployment insurance, and to a lesser extent, welfare payments. (I believe that
  in most countries, the spending on "welfare" is slower moving
  than the cycle, as it takes time to qualify.) The money is flow-
  ing *only* to households where they have lost work, and so it is
  targeted only at areas where unemployment is rising. On the
  flip side, taxes are generally imposed mainly via income taxes and value-added taxes (outside the United States), and so
  people losing jobs and spending less also reduces the aggregate

---

and Matthew C. Klein) for raising the point of residential mortgages when
I discussed this topic on that platform.

35   Using credit controls to target regions is probably going to be
more effective to slow down overheating regions than boost weak ones.
If a region or industry is facing falling incomes, banks are not going to
rush to lend to them, even if their lending cap is increased. This is because
credit controls put limits on lending aggregates, but there is no obvious
mechanism to force banks to lend to particular entities.

tax bill in a targeted manner. (In an online conversation, Eric Lonergan raised the concern that automatic stabilisers are not considered "fiscal policy" in some quarters. I would argue that this point of view makes sense from the perspective of central bankers (for example) – since discussing changes to welfare state programmes is normally outside their domain – but not in the context that I am using here. The parameters of welfare state programmes are fiscal in nature and set by policymakers.)

The use of the terms "targeted" and "non-targeted" suggests my bias: I am in the camp that prefers targeted measures. There is a long line of critiques of non-targeted measures, which I will return to shortly. It would be unfair to argue that economists who discuss "non-targeted" fiscal policy do not understand the advantage of targeting. They would likely respond that it is difficult to expand such targeted measures, so they do not emphasise them. Furthermore, the belief that policymakers can optimally steer the economy – an offshoot of the optimal control theory fad that took hold in the 1960s – has not completely died in some quarters.

Other than the Job Guarantee proposed by Modern Monetary Theory, there are not too many additional avenues to expand the list of possible targeted welfare state programmes. Although increasing the generosity of welfare state programmes in many developed countries seems politically and economically feasible, we should not expect such steps to abolish the business cycle completely. One quick justification of that assertion is that welfare state programmes were generally stronger in the 1950s-1970s, and recessions were arguably more frequent in many of the developed countries. I will return to this point further, below, in my discussion of the Job Guarantee proposal.

There is a long history of criticism of aggregate demand management. Hyman Minsky discussed problems with the old Keynesian policies in the 1960s; the essays reprinted in *Ending Poverty: Jobs, Not Welfare*[36] provide an overview of his thinking. From a theoretical perspective, his complaint was that we need to disaggregate the labour force, and that aggregate demand policies ended up stimulating the higher-wage members of the work force (labourers who were either more skilled or fit the

36   *Ending Poverty: Jobs, Not Welfare*, by Hyman P. Minsky, Levy Economics Institute, 2013. ISBN: 978-1-936192-30-4.

biases of employers). The increase in demand did not trickle down to the most disadvantaged, and in-demand workers faced large demand. This helped create an inflationary bias in the economy – in demand workers were able to push through wage increases – even though aggregate employment was relatively soft (since there was relatively high unemployment among low demand workers). I would note that this explanation of "stagflation" – the combination of high unemployment and inflation, defying the Phillips Curve – appears to have very little to do with the consensus neoclassical narrative about stagflation. (I will not pursue this discussion, as I wish to defer the discussion of inflation to another book.)

U.S.: Percentage Of Unemployed That Are Long-Term Unemployed*

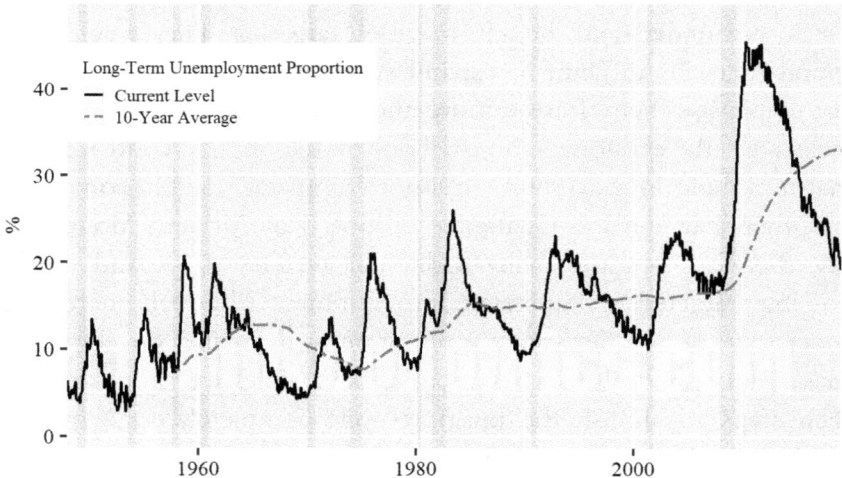

*Greater than 27 weeks. Shade indicats NBER recessions. Source: BLS (via FRED).

Long-term unemployment in the United States

For a more recent take on the subject, Pavlina R. Tcherneva wrote "Reorienting Fiscal Policy: A Critical Assessment of Fiscal Fine-Tuning" in 2013.[37] She outlines the criticism of aggregate demand management policies from the perspective of Modern Monetary Theory, which continues the arguments made by Hyman Minsky. Once again,

37   "Reorienting Fiscal Policy: A Critical Assessment of Fiscal Fine-Tuning," by Pavlina R. Tcherneva, Levy Economics Institute Working Paper Number 772, 2013. URL: http://www.levyinstitute.org/pubs/wp_772.pdf

the argument is that the labour market needs to be disaggregated.

The previous figure depicts one of the empirical problems she observes in the report: the secular increase in long-term unemployment as a share of the total. The percentage of the total unemployed that have been unemployed for at least 27 weeks jumps in each recession, and the minimum reached in each cycle has risen during the recessions after the 1970s. That is, there is a decreasing inability for a segment in the unemployed to escape that fate; dynamism in the labour segment is fading. The argument is that policy is tilted against such people: they are exhorted to find jobs, yet no effort is made to ensure that jobs exist for them to take.

The argument from MMT is that policy needs to be skewed towards the disadvantaged to reduce the divergences in the labour market. This is presumed to have less of an inflationary effect, since there is less stimulus of the higher wage cohorts. The preferred MMT policy proposal – creating a Job Guarantee that ensures that all workers have access to a job at a fixed wage – is precisely targeted at this cohort. The Job Guarantee wage acts as a *de facto* minimum wage, but its level will not greatly influence remuneration at higher incomes, much as is the case currently with minimum wage laws.

The Tcherneva article explains how this critique of policy is tied to the MMT critique of the world-view provided by neoclassical models. Since I am deferring the subject to another book, the reader may wish to pursue the analysis therein.

Reactive, Not Proactive?

Although I believe that the Job Guarantee is a better policy framework, it is not enough to *prevent* recessions. Since private sector wages will be set at a markup over the Job Guarantee wage, anyone losing a private sector job would most likely have an after-tax income reduction when they transition to the Job Guarantee. As such, consumer demand will fall, as can private investment. As a result, output will drop, even if there is technically no increase in unemployment. (Since the Job Guarantee is a form of employment, people in the programme would not be "unemployed" under standard definitions. However, under the assumption that popular unemployment insurance schemes are also left in place,[38] there would likely be a rise in the measured unemployment rate.)

38   Unemployment insurance seems redundant if a Job Guarantee

In other words, the Job Guarantee will soften the blow of a recession for workers but will not prevent them from happening. Firms with shaky business plans will still be weeded out.

I would note that if one attaches great significance to expectations and their interaction with the business cycle, that downcast assessment might need to be amended. One could argue that the expectation of a strong auto-stabiliser will cause firms to rationally not cut back on investments in a coordinated fashion. This prevents recessions, other than fluctuations caused by "extreme bad luck" with respect to pesky "external shocks." However, such beliefs about the self-reinforcing nature of expectations do not seem to be borne out by observed data (since recessions do in fact occur in welfare states). As a result, I will not pursue that argument further.

Sahm Rule as a Proactive Response?

In the article "Direct Stimulus Payments to Individuals" (initially described in Section 2.5), Claudia Sahm proposed what others have referred to as "the Sahm Rule." The rule can be summarised as a direct payment to individuals triggered when the unemployment rate rises beyond a threshold. (The 3-month moving average rising by 0.5% over its minimum of the previous year was the threshold proposed for the United States.)

(To be clear, Sahm's policy proposal is not being suggested as a method to *prevent* recessions. Since the unemployment rate would have already risen by 0.5%, a recession may already have occurred. However, one could imagine some econometric tweaking to the rule that could result in a slightly faster reaction time, and hypothetically prevent recessions. Since nobody is proposing such a rule right now, I am discussing the Sahm proposal as the closest approximation of such a hypothetical proactive rule.)

Sahm's arguments are based on analysis of consumer behaviour in response to stimulus payments in previous recessions. Consumers were more likely to spend out of one-time grants of cash than they would for repeat-exists. However, unemployment insurance schemes typically have benefits tied to previous wages. For example, at the time of writing, payments in Canada are 55% of insurable earnings, with a cap: https://www.canada.ca/en/services/benefits/ei/ei-regular-benefit/benefit-amount.html. Meanwhile, not being required to work on a Job Guarantee job to get benefits makes job searching easier. The path of least political resistance is to leave both systems in place.

ed small payments. As a result, she advocates a single payment, with only a possibility of payments a year later (assuming continued weakness). The suggested size was a payment that results in a total cost of 0.7% of GDP.

Since I believe that the use of fiscal policy is preferable to relying on monetary policy to stimulate the economy[39], I have some sympathies for the policy. The positive factors I see are as follows.

- Relatively easy to set up from a political perspective, but I think the politics are a net negative once we factor in the reaction I expect from politicians and political commentators (discussed below). This is aided by the fact that it is being sold as an automated decision rule – which is the preference of "mainstream" economists (although not my personal preference, but I know that I would be in the minority).
- Since the premise is that the transfer is equal for citizens, it would help flatten income inequality and ensure that there is a higher propensity to consume out of it. (A tax cut presumes one is paying taxes, and the amount that can be cut is going to be in some sense proportional to taxes you pay. As a result, tax cuts can end up being slanted towards households with a lower propensity to spend the proceeds, lowering the effective multiplier.)
- Since the payment is not tied to the amount of money paid in unemployment benefits (etc.), the amount can be larger than what is implied by job losses. This means we could have a larger effective response than what is possible solely from automatic stabilisers.

Unfortunately, I see several negative factors, which means I would not make a major push in the policy's favour.

- Recessions now seem to happen only once per decade. Building an administrative infrastructure that sends out cheques once every ten years could be questioned, but those objections now look much weaker after the events of 2020. (I was critical of

---

39   To be clear, my views about monetary policy are not symmetric. Rapid rate hikes have a proven ability to cause stress in the private sector, and presumably induce a recession. This means that central banks do have the ability to enforce a cap on inflation – if we are willing to accept ugly economic outcomes. Instead, I question the ability of central banks to induce an acceleration in inflation but cutting rates.

the suggestion on this basis, but it can now be sold as a way to be ready for events similar to the pandemic of 2020.) As Sahm notes, the issue is that governments are in the business of taking in tax payments from everyone, but currently most governments do not make universal payments. We cannot just reverse the income tax flows, since adults who are below the income tax threshold pay no taxes, nor do they even need to file a tax return (in Canada, at least). Unless tax payments are being made by withholding, the tax authorities may not even know your current address – they only would find out when you file. (This lack of information may not be true for all developed countries; so, the importance of that point varies.) As such, the government needs to build a secure system to make such payments, which then needs to be updated as information technology systems keep evolving. However, if the programme is sold as being part of a national security/anti-pandemic strategy, these costs might be easily accepted by the broad public.

- Most of the payments will be sent to households that have not yet experienced job losses (unless it is a rapid-moving depression), and so the stimulus will likely be hitting regions that are not yet weak. It seems difficult to worry about stagflation at the time of writing, but this would be unwelcomed in an environment with more inflationary pressures. (Stagflation is the experience of slow growth coupled with rising inflationary pressures.)
- The bias towards rules-based policy by mainstream economists makes them too easily dismiss the fact that elected politicians can do a good job every so often. The immediate response by fiscal authorities to the Financial Crisis was broadly correct; at most, one could argue that stimulus plans could have been larger. By not blindly applying a rule, expenditures can be targeted at the obvious points of weakness. If politicians instead rely on the intervention by technocrats, they may fool themselves into believing that they need do nothing else to respond.
- Fiscal conservatives will be fiscally conservative. Although a stimulus package of 0.7% of GDP is not that big a package to throw at a typical recession, that is not how it would

be reported in the business press. For the current American economy, the usual tactic would be to argue that the government is spending \$147,000,000,000! Since fiscal deficits will be blowing out by even larger amounts, there would be immediate calls to cut spending on social programmes in order to avoid a "financial crisis" caused by "bond vigilantes." This highly predictable reaction blows up the entire premise of rules-based policy, since the cuts to social programmes are likely to cripple the recovery, as the countries that pushed austerity policies in the post-2010 period discovered the hard way.

Forward-Looking (Discretionary) Policy?

If we wanted to prevent recessions with fiscal policy, we need policymaking to be more forward-looking. I am not too enthusiastic about the prospects for such a policy framework.

If we accept my premise that recessions are hard to forecast, it is obviously going to be difficult to forestall them with fiscal policy (whether we attempt to apply a rule or use policymaker discretion). For example, I launched my website six years earlier than this text was written. I do not attempt to forecast the economy, but I do comment on the current situation. For almost the entire period I have been writing, I have felt that it was almost always necessary to include disclaimers about potential recession risks. To be fair to my own forecasting abilities, I was not forecasting a recession, rather I was noting that there were plausible stories about recession risks. If one examines financial market data, we did see periodic episodes that might be viewed as incipient recession scares (the inversion in yield curves that started in 2018 being the strongest such episode). Since pro-active policy cannot wait until a recession is clearly underway, I would argue that in the counter-factual world of discretionary pro-active recession prevention, we would have had at least one round of fiscal stimulus in that six-year period – even though no recession occurred (putting aside the uncertain status of the latest scare, which is coincident with my writing of the manuscript).

If we couple this to the Minsky/Tcherneva critiques of aggregate demand management, we could see that this might impart an inflationary bias to policy. Admittedly, growth in the developed economies has been so sluggish that the inflation risks would have been quite small. (For example, the tax cuts from the Trump administration did little to raise inflation – yet.)

Correspondingly, my view is that we should set our sights slightly lower than preventing recessions. Instead, many developed countries should improve the safety net to better shelter workers from economic volatility (the business sector is very good at taking care of itself) and rely on the instincts of politicians to react to downturns in a sensible fashion. If central banks wish to attempt to prevent recessions with monetary policy, they are welcome to try. However, I am unconvinced about the plausibility of such efforts, which I will discuss in Volume II, where I will look at monetary policy in greater depth.

Chapter 4 **Post-Keynesian Real Business Cycle Theory**

4.1   Introduction

We now turn to post-Keynesian analysis of business cycles. These theories can be quite complex, with a great many interrelated factors. In order to simplify discussions, I will draw a line between the real economy and the financial aspects of the business cycle. (The *real economy* refers to the nonfinancial aspects of the economy: such as production, employment and the associated income flows.) It should be underlined that this is purely my preference on how to present the material; post-Keynesians normally emphasise that the real and financial aspects of the economy are interrelated (and complain about neoclassical models that eliminate financial considerations).

A recession is inherently a real economy phenomenon, since it is a contraction in real output. Disruptions in the financial markets that do not carry over to the real economy are not the topic of discussion. For example, an equity bear market will cause great excitement in the business press, yet does not qualify as a recession.

The usual way in which a contraction is triggered is by a contraction in fixed investment. Firms invest because they have optimistic forecasts about future demand; anything that dampens that enthusiasm will cause a retrenchment in investment. Disruptions in the financial markets typically accentuate the contraction in fixed investment, but not all disruptions will result in such a follow through. Meanwhile, the disruption in financial markets is often related to the underlying developments in the real economy, and so we need to understand why the real economy will drift away from orderly growth on its own.

4.2   Kalecki Profit Equation

The Kalecki profit equation – named after the economist Michal Kalecki – describes how aggregated profits are determined by national accounting identities. (Note that Jerome Levy came up with a similar approach earlier; the equation is sometimes referred to as the Kalecki-Levy profit equation.) The results are perhaps not obvious if we look at profits from a bottom up perspective. From the perspective of business cycle analysis, the key point to note is that net investment is a source of profits. Meanwhile, since firms invest in order to grow profits, we get a self-reinforcing feedback loop. From a policy perspective, we see that governmental deficits also add to profits, which implies that increasing deficits add to profits in a recession, helping put a floor under activity.

If we wanted to apply the profit equation to real world national accounts data, the final equation contains a great number of terms. This complexity distracts from the basic principles of the equation. Instead, this treatment will start off with the equation for very simple model economies, and then add terms as we add complexity to the models. The usefulness of the Kalecki profit equation is for understanding the model dynamics that transfer to real world behaviour, rather than playing with national accounts identities. We can build up the equation term-by-term, and so we can have an intuition of the role of each term.

This treatment is largely based on the one found in Section 5.3.6 of Marc Lavoie's *Post-Keynesian Economics: New Foundations*. I would also note the historical discussion found in "Profits: The Views of Jerome Levy and Michal Kalecki" by S. Jay Levy.[40] Levy's analysis tended to be more focused on the details of the national accounts. The simplicity of Kalecki's exposition probably explains why his name is used in naming the relationship.

Model 1: Simplest Two-Sector Model

We will start with the simplest case: an economic model with just two sectors (the business sector and workers), and no investment. Furthermore, we will assume that the business sector does not pay dividends. In order to eliminate investment, we will assume that the business either provides services or highly perishable goods; there are no inventories. We will refer to this as Model 1, and it has an associated profit equation.

We will treat the business sector as if it were a single employer. If there are multiple employers, we might see that some are profitable and others run at a loss; what we are interested in is aggregate profit, so the distribution across firms does not matter.

The business sector's profits are equal to revenue minus expenses.

- Revenue equals purchases by households.

40   URL: http://www.levyinstitute.org/pubs/wp309.pdf

- Expenses are equal to wages paid to workers.

We can immediately see that if households spend exactly the amount of their wages, revenue equals expenses and profits are equal to zero. There is a circular flow of cash out of the firm to workers which then returns as revenue, and no cash drops out of the loop. However, if workers save some of their income, revenue will be less than expenses; cash has dropped out of the loop. This gives us a version of the profit equation with just one term:

(Model 1 Profits) = - (Household savings).

Even this simplest version of the profit equation has a couple interesting theoretical properties.

The first thing to note is that since household savings subtract from profits, rising savings "all else equal" has a negative cyclical effect. Variants of this concept show up throughout discussions of simple monetary models; for example, the desire to hoard money could allegedly lead to a recession. However, there does not seem to be any evidence of such an effect in market economic analysis. From my perspective, the emphasis on household savings as a cyclical factor by academic economists caused me to view their work as being unrealistic. The problem is the overly simplified near-barter economies academics use to illustrate their models. The issue in practice is not changes in what households view as "saving," rather the willingness to incur debt. By having some households borrowing more than is saved by others, the savings of the household sector ends up negative, allowing for positive profits.

Within this two-sector model, there are two avenues to allow this borrowing.

1. The business sector can lend to households; for example, by offering financing on purchases. The business sector could end up with an unchanged cash balance, but it will gain financial assets – the debt-like claims emitted by the household sector.
2. Individual households can lend to other households. However, this can only be sustained for as long as lending households hold cash instruments.[41]

---

41   These sorts of complicated intra-sector transactions can break overly simplistic analysis that wants to develop mechanistic models of cash flows in the economy. Because of things like intra-sector borrowing, measured gross debt levels can move around without resulting in changes in

Household consumption patterns appear to be relatively stable across the cycle (during the expansion, at least). However, the willingness to incur debts is more cyclical, particularly with respect to housing and car purchases.[42] We need to drop the parables about Farmer Bob buying apples from Farmer Alicia, or Bob's desire to hold gold coins, rather the issue is whether their kids Cynthia and Doug are buying a condo in the big city.

The next thing to note is that one could view the equation as implying that household frugality is a negative. This is in stark contrast to the conventional story that we need to increase household savings to boost growth. ("Farmer Bob needs to hold back some of his corn to plant next year!") It should be noted that this model stacks the deck against frugality by assuming that investment is zero; I will return to this when investment is added to the model.

Model 2: Dividends

The next addition to the model is dividends. Neoclassical models have a hard time with dividends, for reasons that will be discussed below. However, the inclusion of dividends in the equation has some major theoretical and political effects on the economy.

A dividend is a payment by a firm to its owners, and dividend income is normally the objective for capitalist firms. The normal assumption is that dividends are paid out of profits (current or historical) – although the private equity industry has mucked that belief up.

Dividends and wages are the two main cash flows from the business sector to the household sector in economic models. (In the real world, some individuals either are self-employed or part of private partnerships that end up being lumped in the household sector in the national accounts. As a result, real world data could see more types of interactions than the tidy world of economic models.) Although the cash flows may be fungible, measured GDP. Conversely, if one assumes that debt is only issued to purchase goods and services, one can incorrectly believe that there is an iron law relating debt changes to GDP changes.

42   The purchase of an existing house does not itself add to GDP, whereas it will inflate household debt (in the typical case where the buyer will end up with a larger mortgage than the seller will). This makes sense, as we do not consider the proceeds of a house sale to be income. That said, there are large income effects in a typical housing transaction.

they have very different implications for profits: dividends are not an expense.

If we assume that the household sector has zero savings, all business cash outflows return in revenue. So, if 20% of outflows are dividends, only 80% of outflows are wages. This means that profits (revenues minus expenses) are 20% of revenue – or equal to the dividend payments. However, the household savings is generally non-zero, and we end up with the profit equation #2, with an added term:

(Model 2 Profits) = - (Household savings) + (Dividend payments).

(That is, we added another term to the equation.)

One typical way to present Kalecki's model is to add some behavioural information that acts to constrain outcomes. One typical assumption (what I term here as the "Kalecki Assumption") is that workers and capitalists are distinct sets of households, and that workers spend 100% of their wages (and do not dis-save). This has the implication that household sector savings are exactly equal to the savings of the households that receive dividends.

This implies a different profit equation:

("Kalecki Assumption Profits") = (Dividend payments) - (Capitalist savings),

which by definition of savings implies:

("Kalecki Assumption Profits") = (Capitalist consumption).

This explains Kaldor's aphorism:[43]

Capitalists earn what they spend, and workers spend what they earn.

Once again, this version of the equation only holds in models with the constraint that workers' aggregate savings are exactly equal to zero; this will not be true in real world data (except as a statistical fluke). Furthermore, since workers and salary owners can also own equities (courtesy of the move to self-directed retirement schemes), we have a blurring in the distinction between "workers" and "capitalists." Nevertheless, it does seem safe to argue that dividend income is largely received by the upper income

---

43   N. Kaldor, "Alternative Theories of Distribution," Review of Economic Studies, 23 (2), pages 83-100. The quote itself is in page 96. I got the reference from Marc Lavoie's *Post-Keynesian Economics: New Foundations*. Lavoie notes that this quotation is often misattributed to Kalecki.

quantiles, and those quantiles have a greater propensity to save. Therefore, the behavioural constraint might be a reasonable approximation of reality.

The addition of the dividend term to the profit equation has limited real world significance in terms of cyclical analysis. Over short spans of time, dividends are stable, and so this term is not too significant a source of volatility when compared to the other terms to be added. Over multi-decade periods, the changes in dividend policy would presumably show up in secular profit trends, and so assertions about the long-term would need to take dividend changes into account. However, the addition of dividends to the profit equation is very important from a theoretical perspective, as well as for political economy.

(The current popularity of stock buybacks might muddy the theoretical waters. In a stock buyback, the business sector outflows are in exchange for financial assets, and the seller will not count the sales proceeds as normal income. At most, there will be capital gains. Trying to analyse this properly would require something like a stock-flow consistent model that takes into account equity market valuations and capital gains. Those models are complex and raise a great number of thorny questions.)

The theoretical problem with dividends being a source of profits is that it creates a self-reinforcing feedback loop between profits and dividends, as greater profits allow for greater dividends. For simpler models like stock-flow consistent models, this is not an issue. However, if one believes that model outcomes are in some sense the result of optimising behaviour, this creates difficulties. If the business sector (or capitalists) were truly aiming for optimal outcomes, the solution would likely be pathological, with extremely high dividends that are not saved. Neoclassical models avoid these problems by avoiding actual optimisations, instead sectors follow heuristics that are sub-optimal relative to choices that are implied by taking into account the full macro model.[44] This accords with my previous experience in applied mathematics: for practical problems, optimisations tend to result in pathological outcomes.

Even if we accept that economic outcomes are not in any sense optimal,

---

44   I described this in an online article "The Curious Notation of DSGE Models." I expect to return to this issue in the second volume. URL: http://www.bondeconomics.com/2018/03/the-curious-notation-of-dsge-models.html

there are important implications of the role of dividends. The implication is that the levels of profits in an economic system are essentially arbitrary; for any level of output, we can split the output between workers and capital and have a system that respects cash flow constraints (accounting identities). An economic model needs to pin down the distribution of income using some assumptions about behaviour in order to have a single solution.

Neoclassical models hide distributional questions under the carpet by assuming that workers and capital receive their just desserts: marginal contributions determine the levels of wages and profits, and hence the income shares. As a result, it is possible to ignore the politics of income distribution. By contrast, the post-Keynesian tradition explicitly notes the arbitrary nature of income distributions. To be fair, "mainstream" economists are now more willing to discuss the effects of income distribution (at least the leftward end of the mainstream).

From a short-term perspective, distributional questions are a second order effect. I have seen arguments to the effect that the structural sluggishness of recent decades is due to a lower wage share of national income, but I am agnostic on the validity of that view. Investment trends are much more important for profit determination, as I discuss next.

Model 3: Investment

Investment is arguably the most important cyclical component during an expansion. For those who are new to economics, one needs to keep in mind that the definition of "investment" in economics does not match the way the word is often commonly used. For example, people will often use "investing in the stock market" as a way of describing the purchase of shares; this does not fit the definition used in economics. Instead, "investment" here refers to spending by firms that creates non-financial assets that presumably will generate future profits. The trick is that this can either be fixed investment, or investment in inventories. The issues around inventory investment will be discussed later.

The usual convention in the national accounts is that investment is largely an activity of the business sector; household spending is usually classified as consumption. This is an artefact of the nature of the way that national accounts are measured. For example, national statisticians cannot tell whether my purchase of a computer is to support consulting activities (an investment) or to play the latest video games (which is a form of consumption). There is also the possibility of investment by the government sector, but we lose very little information for the discussion here if we lump that in with business investment. The discussion here follows the convention that only the business sector invests.

Investment is another cash outflow by businesses that is not an expense. As a result, circular flows result in revenue that is not matched by a wage expense – profits.

The Model 3 equation now reads:

(Model 3 Profits) = (Net Investment) - (Household savings) + (Dividend payments).

The transactions for investment are more complicated than the previous models. We can imagine three basic channels for investment in this simplified framework. (If we add more sectors, there are more possibilities.)

1. The firm pays workers $100 to create a capital good. The $100 payment is not treated as an expense, it is instead "capitalised." From the workers' perspective, it does not make a difference whether the $100 is expensed or not; it is a household income-producing cash flow that can be spent. The household cash flow then recirculates through the system as before. Profits are higher since we are now no longer deducting some of the cash flows from revenue.

2. The firm pays workers $100 to produce products that are not sold. The unsold products will end up in inventory. The inventory will be held on the balance sheet at the production cost (which is equal to wage payments needed to produce the goods). The hope is that the goods in inventory will be sold in a future accounting period, and the profits on the sale are equal to the sales price less the cost of the goods as valued in inventory. (Under most circumstances firms cannot mark the value of inventories as equal to their final selling price, as firms could generate "profits" by just producing goods that cannot be sold and dumping them into inventory.) This then leads to another observation – selling the goods out of inventory represents disinvestment (negative investment), and this amount would be subtracted from gross investment in the next accounting period

to get net investment. (Note that the profit equation specifies net investment, not gross investment.)

3. Firm A purchases a capital good for $100 from Firm B. Firm B held the good in inventory, with a value of $80. The $100 cash outflow for Firm A is not an expense; and so, the transaction is profit neutral. For Firm B, the profit on the transaction is equal to the selling price ($100) less the cost of goods sold ($80) – which implies a profit of $20. The net investment for the aggregate business sector is also $20. Firm A has a new fixed investment of $100, while Firm B has an inventory disinvestment of $80. It is easy to see that cash flows can get quite complicated once we allow for intra-sector cash flows (e.g., business to business flows). For example, an investment project could have a mixture of purchased inputs as well as worker pay. The key is that investment creates outflows that are not matched to an expense.

Depreciation adds another wrinkle to the concept of net investment. Most capital goods have a finite lifespan, and their value is written down over time. The decrease in asset value is known as depreciation, and it shows up as an expense (the cost of capital). Depreciation is subtracted from other investment in order to get net investment. That is,

Net Investment = (Gross fixed investment) - (Depreciation) + (New goods added to inventory) - (Value of goods sold from inventory).

If we had a static economy with fixed nominal prices, depreciation expense would converge to equal gross investment. For example, assume that all capital goods depreciate by 10% of their initial value every year for 10 years. If firms invest $100 per year, that would create an expense of $10 per year for 10 years. After doing this for 10 years, the level of depreciation expenses would equal the new investment. However, the usual condition for modern economies (outside Japan) is that prices and volumes of investment are rising over time, so the new investment is larger than the depreciation of earlier investments (which have a lower nominal value).

The net investment component of the profit equation is much more important from a cyclical perspective than household saving and dividends. The reason is that investment is pro-cyclical: firms invest if they expect higher future demand – and profits. Since investment itself generates profits, expectations of higher profits can be viewed as self-fulfilling. This means that expansion is the natural state for capitalism; the problem is that other factors can derail profits and investment, and then the self-reinforcing feedback depresses activity.

I would summarise the post-Keynesian view of how firms operate during an expansion as follows. It is a mistake to believe that firms attempt to solve some optimisation problem in order to plan their activities; they are missing too much useful information to fill in the optimisation parameters. Instead, they need to use rules of thumb (heuristics), such as extrapolating past growth trends. Obviously, they do a great deal of analysis of their market, but there is an obvious great amount of uncertainty about the direction of the overall economy. They will then come up with some baseline forecast of demand for their products.

They will plan production to meet demand, and to grow their inventories in line with sales. That is, they typically want to keep the ratio of inventory to sales at some target ratio, such as holding one month's sales in inventory. (Since inventory is a stock and sales are a flow, the ratio has units of time.)

They will launch fixed investments if they believe that they need to add capacity to meet projected demand.

The implication is that if firms are projecting demand growth over their planning horizon, they will generally plan on both increasing inventories as well as increasing fixed investment.

The future does not always meet past projections. Two competing firms may have ramped up capacity beyond the demand for their products, and so sales end up below their projections. If they are producing goods that are held in inventory, they will end up with a higher inventory-to-sales ratio than desired. By itself, the higher inventory levels do not cause a loss. However, the unplanned inventory build represents a hit to cash flow – they paid cash to produce the inventory. Their balance sheet weightings shift from cash to inventories – and they need cash to meet expenses and repay debts. The inventory build must be reversed – which implies a reduction in investment.

This means that "investment" is not an unalloyed positive, as it is sometimes portrayed in economic parables. One very often encounters stories about Robinson Crusoe economies, or economies that consist of barter among various sole proprietors (fisherman, shoemakers, etc.). In such an exchange economy, investment is represented as frugally abstaining from consuming output to add to productive capacity. However, in a monetary economy, "investment" may just be the piling up of unsold goods at firms – and those firms will go bankrupt if that inventory build is not reversed. This explains the Keynesian emphasis on the role of demand within the economy.

Model 4: Government Fiscal Policy

We now add in a government sector to the model, to create Model #4. To recapitulate, the previous state of the equation is:

(Model 3 Profits) = (Net Investment) - (Household savings) + (Dividend payments).

The addition of the government sector changes the equation to:

(Model 4 Profits) = (Net Investment) - (Household savings) + (Dividend payments) + (Government Fiscal Deficit).

The addition of the government sector added the final term to the equation – the fiscal deficit. This is a conventional phrasing, but it must be kept in mind that the fiscal deficit is the negative of the fiscal balance, so we need to flip signs if we want to use the fiscal balance as the variable. The usual condition for governments is to run deficits, so it is more familiar to express the equation using it.

The reason why a fiscal deficit creates profits is that the government is now injecting cash into the circular flows in the economy. If the government mails a senior a $100 transfer payment, and said senior immediately runs out and spends it, thist represents $100 in business sector revenue that is not matched to any wage expenses.

(I am following the convention of economic models and treating government spending as consumption. If governments capitalised some investment expenditures, those expenditures might not be considered part of the fiscal deficit, instead they would show up in the net investment term. As a result, the reclassification is a wash from a profit perspective, although the handling of the depreciation of governmental fixed assets will also need to be accounted for.)

For profits, the full fiscal balance matters, not just the primary balance (the fiscal balance excluding interest payments). Conventional economic analysis often likes to focus on the primary balance, but this glosses over the reality that interest payments by the government are an income source to the non-governmental sector.

The presence of the fiscal deficit in the profit equation is an important part of the counter-cyclical nature of fiscal policy. In a recession, deficits naturally grow – the tax take falls, while welfare state spending (such as unemployment insurance) automatically increases. Furthermore, even fiscal conservatives tend to panic in a downturn, adding active stimulus measures to the mix. The rising contribution of the fiscal deficit will counteract the drop in private sector investment, putting a floor under profits (and animal spirits) in the private sector.

During an expansion, fiscal deficits tend to contract (or least grow less than GDP in nominal terms). This acts as an increasing drag on profits, counteracting the pro-cyclical impetus from investment.

Model 5: The External Sector

The final addition to the profit equation is to bring in the external sector (imports and exports). If a country has net imports of goods, it implies that net cash flows are heading to foreign entities – implying a loss in the circular flow of income.

The addition of the external sector adds a new wrinkle – the profits that we are discussing here are domestic profits, which is not the same thing as national profits. A local firm may have profits in its foreign subsidiaries, but those will not show up in the domestic national accounts. A stock market investor is interested in the total profits of firms, and not just domestic profits, so the distinction needs to be kept in mind.

(Model 5 Profits) = (Net Investment) - (Household savings) + (Dividend payments) + (Government Fiscal Deficit) - (Net Imports).

The breakage in cash flows is straightforward. If a worker spends $100 on imported goods out of wage income, the source of the wages was an expense to the domestic business sector, while the domestic sector gains no revenue.

This raises a different perspective on the question of protectionism. From the perspective of optimising decisions of households, free trade is an obvious advantage, as it opens the opportunity set for consumption purposes. However, a trade deficit is a negative for domestic corporate profits.

If we assume that imports as a percentage of total domestic consumption is stable (the propensity to import), import growth will equal the domestic growth rate. Meanwhile, exports would tend to grow at the growth rate of export markets. The implication is that if our domestic growth rate is greater than elsewhere, the trade balance will tend to decrease (e.g., become more negative). For the "Anglo" countries (such as the United

States) in recent decades, trade deficits will tend to rise during an expansion. (That is to say, growth is not "export-led," which is the case for some economies, both developed and developing.) As a result, the external sector will tend to act in a stabilising fashion for profits. This will be less true for countries following an export-led growth dynamic, as the persistent trade surplus will tend to move in tandem with the global business cycle.

Summary

We have slowly built up the Kalecki Profit equation to a general form. We would need to adapt it to take into accounts various technicalities in the national accounts if we wanted to apply it to real world data. I am unconvinced about the value of such an exercise, since it is unlikely that we could forecast each of the components of the full equation. Meanwhile, if we are not interested in forecasting, we can just read off profits from the national accounts, rather than calculating them with an accounting identity. Instead, the value of the accounting identity is for the analysis of models and getting a high-level understanding of the nature of the dynamics.

For example, one notes that the wage bill does not appear in the equation. That is, rising wages are not necessarily a negative for profits – which is not obvious if we pursue a bottom up microeconomic perspective. Rising wages would presumably allow for greater household savings (which does appear in the equation), but that is a second order effect.

However, the most important take away is the importance of investment for the business cycle. Businesses invest on the expectation of greater future profits – and investment is a source of aggregate profits. Central banks playing around with the money supply is at most a speed bump in the way of the self-reinforcing growth dynamics of industrial capitalism.

From a policy perspective, Minsky argued that this accounting logic implies the need for a relatively large central government to tame the business cycle. Small governments (5-10% of GDP, which was relatively normal peacetime share pre-World War II) will not generate a large enough cyclical swing in the fiscal deficit to cancel out the fixed investment cycle. The absence of the automatic stabilisers explains the tendencies of earlier economies to experience depressions, and not just recessions.

4.3   The Inevitability of Debt Finance for Private Investment

One needs to be careful about the effects of aggregation in models. For example, one might be misled by the implications of the Kalecki Profit Equation (discussed in the previous section). The equation suggests that private investment is self-financing, since investment is a source of profits. This is true in aggregate, but the reality is that the firms that increase investment are not necessarily the ones with increased profits. The financial system is required to bridge financing flows between these firms.

Alternatively, when we look at the economy, it is characterised by circular flows: one entity's outgo is another entity's income (using "income" loosely, really any cash flow). This is what allows upward spirals in nominal debt outstanding: there is no "law of nature" to stop debt growth. The tendency for money outflows to return to the source because of these circular flows is known as *reflux*. For a large entity like a central bank or central government Treasury, these reflux effects are important, and need to be considered when discussing policy. However, for a private sector entity, the reflux effect is generally going to be small, and safely ignored. Even if we ignore the special nature of central government finances (as discussed in *Understanding Government Finance*), the importance of reflux flows means that government finance is not like household finance.

Example

We can now examine an example to see how disaggregation matters. For simplicity, we will just look at the flows between a few private sector entities, leaving out complications like inventories and dividends.

- Assume that there are three firms, A, B, and C, and each pays its workers $100 in the accounting period to produce goods.
- The workers spend all wage income, buying $150 of consumer goods from firms A and B. This gives each of the firms a profit of $50, which is $150 revenue less the wage bill used to produce the goods ($100).
- Meanwhile, both A and B buy $100 worth of capital goods produced by firm C. The purchase of capital goods is a cash flow drain, but it is not an expense in the current accounting period. (The capital would be depreciated, which will be a non-

cash expense in future accounting periods.) The net result of the cash flows for A and B is that each has an outflow of $50 in cash instruments.

- Firm C sells $200 worth of capital goods, with a production cost of $100, leaving a profit of $100. Since we assume that Firm C supplies its own investment goods, it has no investment outflows. The cash inflow matches the level of profits, or $100.

The aggregate profit for the business sector is $200 ($50 each by A and B, and $100 for C). This matches the cut down Kalecki Profit Equation: investment is $200, household savings is $0, and we have excluded all other terms from consideration. Although aggregate profits match aggregate investment, the firms doing the investing had a total cash outflow of $100. They could finance the investment by either transferring existing cash holdings, or more likely, issuing debt instruments.

Since firms cannot run down cash levels forever, the usual mode of financing is to issue debt. This could be done via vendor financing: firm C lends A and B the cash to buy the capital goods.

Vendor Financing versus Other Modes

Vendor financing is a typical way of financing non-capital goods, since we can treat accounts payable as a form of debt instrument. The implication is that the non-financial sector can bypass the financial sector for financing needs.

There are limits to vendor financing. Most fixed capital investments are too large to be safely financed via vendor financing, as that would pose excessive risk to the firm providing the financing (as the telecom sector discovered the hard way in the late 1990s). Therefore, most large investments are financed by long-term debt contracts intermediated by the financial sector. Although banks traditionally did such financing, the changing nature of the financial system has meant that much of the financing has migrated to the bond markets. (There are also cultural differences; for example, German business lending is more bank-oriented than is the case in the United States, which relies more non-bank finance.)

Of course, large profitable firms can self-finance. To the extent that the economy is dominated by established conglomerates, this would reduce the need for external debt financing. Nevertheless, the tendency is for relatively speculative investment to be undertaken by rising firms that are challenging incumbents. Meanwhile, business schools have taught the current generation of corporate managers that a highly indebted capital structure is optimal; firms no longer attempt to defend a triple-A credit rating.

Breakdown in Aggregation

The tendency for investment to be financed by challenger firms also raises issues with aggregate debt statistics. If profitable established firms are paying down debt while new firms are borrowing large amounts to finance speculative profits, the riskiness of business sector debt will be rising even if the aggregate amount of debt outstanding is falling. Analysts would need access to micro-data – such as tracking the universe of debt issuers – to determine whether the risk profile of debt is changing.

From a modelling perspective, the breakdown in aggregation is a problem for approaches that are based on behavioural approaches to the aggregate, such as assuming that profits are maximised. For example, if we assumed that the business sector was in aggregate maximising profits (somehow), the aggregate behaviour would take advantage of the self-financed nature of investment. Stock-flow consistent (SFC) models avoid degenerate behaviour by using heuristics that are based on average behaviour. Agent-based models are disaggregated, and so can capture the range of possible outcomes. (The difficulty with agent-based models is fitting them to data, which is aggregated.)

Equity?

Equity financing is an alternative to debt financing, and so it might appear possible to break the link between investment growth and debt growth. However, the use of equity financing is limited in modern practice, for a number of reasons.

- The premise of equity markets is that investors are targeting a common (risk-adjusted) rate of return on equity. However, the rate of return on assets is much more variable, and lower, than this target. The use of debt financing allows firms to equalise (risk-adjusted) rates of return via magnifying the return on assets via leverage. Since interest payments are taxed and dividends are not, the tax system helps incentivise the use of debt financing.[45]

---

45   For example, imagine an asset with a value of $100 that has a return of 6%. If 50% of the asset is financed at an interest rate of 5%, then

- Debt instruments have finite terms, allowing firms to match financing to the economic lifespan of assets.
- Housing is generally financed by mortgages. It is unclear what entity would be willing to become a junior partner in the equity of homes, nor would homeowners welcome interference from such a partner.
- The credit markets (including the banking sector) have the capacity to match up the portfolio allocation desires of the private sector and debt issuance. The private sector is trapped in a web of nominal obligations (household bills, wage contracts) even if their balance sheet is clean; they want to hold cash instruments to match those outflows. Equity has a highly uncertain value, and so cannot be the entirety of private sector portfolios.

It is possible that equity will be a more important source of finance in the future. However, this would require changing attitudes within society, such as somehow lowering the target rate of return on equity. Until then, debt will tend to be correlated with investment.

Role of the Financial System

We can now turn to the role of the financial system. Many popular discussions of finance assume that the role of the financial system is to increase the stock of saving to raise investment. This is a flawed application of loanable funds thinking. The role of the financial system is to allocate financial flows: match savers to borrowers and have pricing on loans properly matched against risks.

We need only look at the well-documented disastrous lending practices during the Financial Crisis to see that the financial system is quite capable of failing to allocate financial flows properly. The post-Keynesian argument is that practices in the financial system are a far more likely cause of (serious) recessions than changes in the real economy, as will be discussed in Chapter 5.

Nevertheless, so long as the financial system is operating in something resembling a normal fashion, borrowers will be able to finance investment at reasonable risk-adjusted rates of interest. The prospects for returns on capital – real economy analysis – can still drive the business cycle. Debt issuance will just move in line with financing require-
the profit is $3.50 (=$6 - $2.5 interest). This implies a rate of return of 7% on the $50 of equity invested.

ments, and so be a *determined* factor, not a *determining* factor for growth.

4.4   A Simple Investment Accelerator Model

One of the basic concepts of Keynesian economics is that real activity is heavily driven by the pace of investment. The household sector is largely a passive actor; shifts in investment activity are the source of economic volatility.

This section outlines a preliminary model of investment, with the financial aspects stripped away. It is a stock-flow consistent (SFC) model, which is built upon the core of the *sfc_models* package, written in the Python programming language. (That package is described in my book, *An Introduction to SFC Models Using Python.*) The code that generates the model has been added to the examples folder of the package.[46]

Model Basics

Although it may have been more sensible to take an existing post-Keynesian model, my preference was to create the simplest possible model with investment. This is for ease of understanding, as well wanted to keep additions to the *sfc_models* package as incremental as possible.

The core of the model is model SIM (for "simplest"), which is found in chapter 3 of Wynne Godley and Marc Lavoie's *Monetary Economics* (and described in chapter 5 of my book). The SIM model has three sectors: households, businesses, and the government. The investment model was created by solely changing the behaviour of the business sector. These changes are inspired by the models that occur in later chapters of *Monetary Economics*.

Readers need to be cautioned that this model would not be considered the best summary of post-Keynesian thinking on the effects of investment. This is a stripped-down model that just looks at the somewhat mechanical income flows that occur between the sectors. Although these income flow effects are enough to generate a moderate business cycle, they are not enough to explain the greater volatility we see in the real world. The introduction of the financing aspects of capital investment will inject greater volatility into the model. The financial effects will be discussed in the next chapter.

Since the model description may be too dry for many readers, I will jump ahead to describe the effects of a jump in private sector investment in the model.

---

46   The package code is available at https://github.com/brianr747/ SFC_models. The file containing the model is *ex201904110_accelerator_gummint.py,* found in the examples/scripts directory.

Short-Run Effects

We are following the convention *of Monetary Economics* and initialise the model up in a no-growth steady state. We then perturb model settings to see the effects on variables.

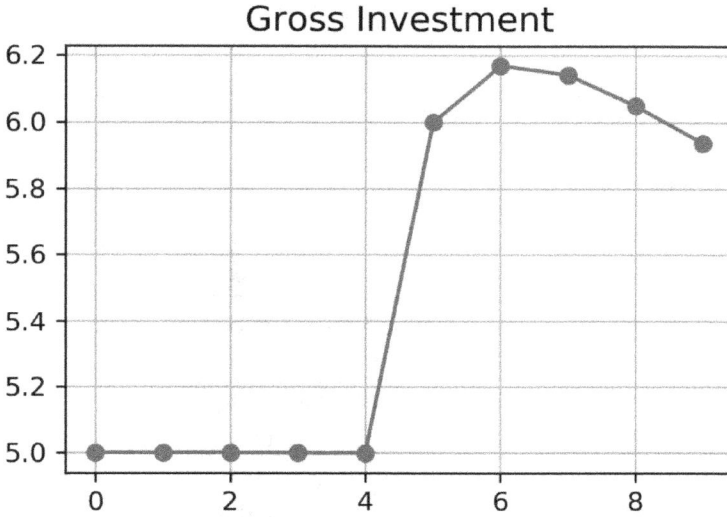

Gross investment in model simulation

In our example, we change the target level of capital in business sector and leave everything else unchanged. The target capital is set as a ratio relative to the size of the employed labour force, and we change the ratio in time period 5. This causes a jump in gross investment in that period (above). In this model, 5% of the capital stock depreciates. With a steady-state capital stock of 100, this means that gross investment of 5 units of output is needed to keep the capital stock unchanged.

Ratio of Capital to Target

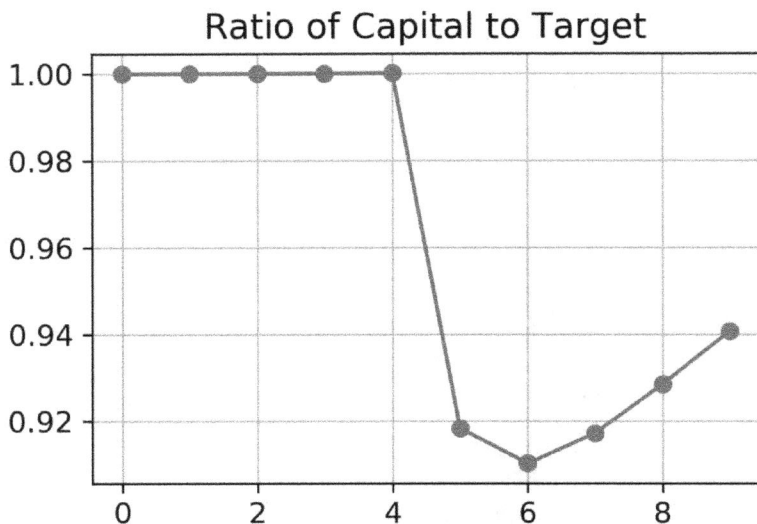

Simulation capital versus target

The adjustment of capital target is not instantaneous. Since the target ratio jumped in time period 5, the ratio of capital to target fell to about 0.92. It then is marching slowly towards its target level during the rest of the sample period.

Wage Income

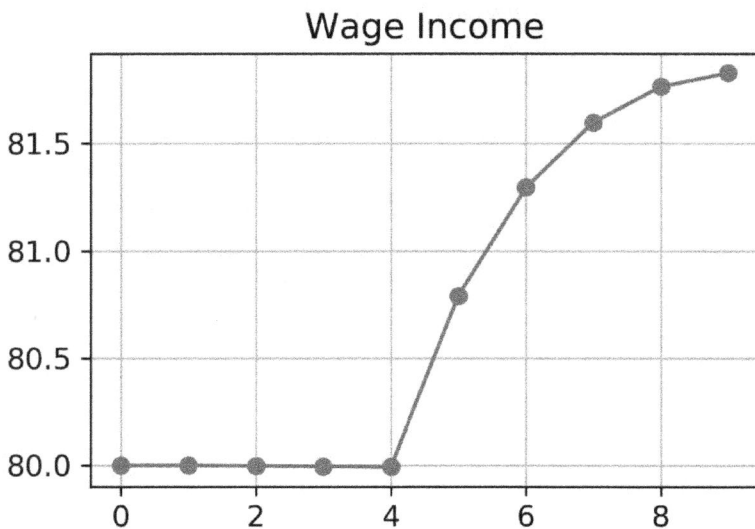

Simulation wage income

In order to increase investment, hiring needs to increase. As seen above, the wage income of the household sector rises from 80 to almost 82 by the end of the sample.

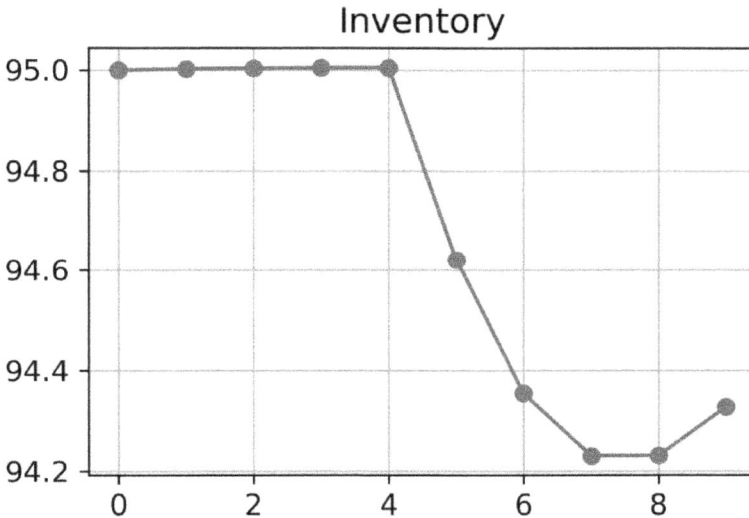

Simulation inventory

An increased wage bill feeds through into greater demand for consumer goods. The business sector uses the previous period's sales as a forecast for the current period (simplest case of adaptive expectations), and as a result, it underestimates demand from the other sectors. (It knows what its own investment plans are.) This forecast miss is accommodated by drawing down inventories. If we wanted to move to greater realism, we would realise that we need to disaggregate the business sector. The firms that increase investment expenditures would most likely not be producing the investment goods themselves, and so the amount of capital goods would be less than demanded as well.

Inventory/Sales Ratio

Simulation inventory-to-sales ratio

As is typical for post-Keynesian models, the business sector follows behavioural conventions. In this case, it has a stock-flow norm: it wants to keep the ratio of inventory (a stock) to sales (a flow) at 1. The underestimate of demand means that this ratio drops below this target level (figure above). As a result, in addition to meeting higher-than-expected demand, it also needs to build inventories. Since inventory builds are a form of investment, we see that total investment ends up being pushed higher by the earlier step up in fixed investment. (Inventory investment will be discussed at greater length in the next section.)

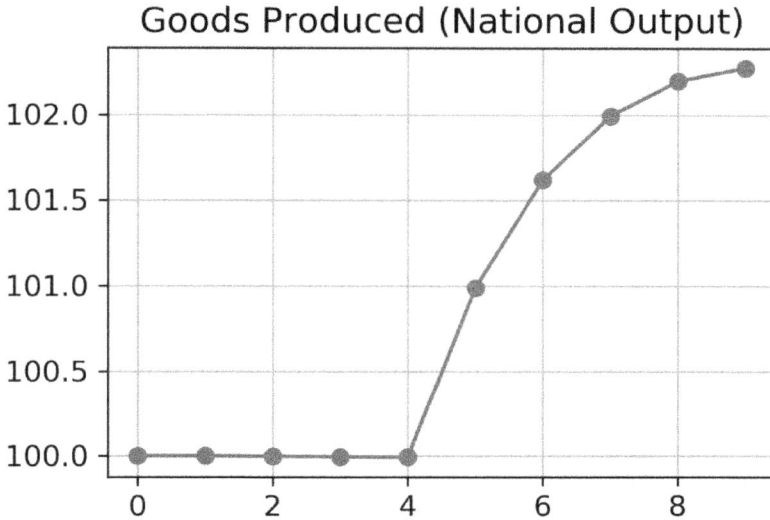

Simulation narional output

The net result of all these forces is depicted above: total production rises from 100 to just over 102 by the end of the sample period. Since fixed investment rose by about 1, we can see that there is a short-term multiplier on investment of about 2. The fact that total output rises by more than the direct impulse of investment explains why fixed investment is a major driver of economic volatility.

Longer Run Effects

If we look at a longer time period (next figure), we see that effects of the change are less one-sided. In fact, we see an oscillation in output. That is, there is a bust after the period of boom. However, the oscillations are damped, and the system converges towards a steady state.

Goods Produced (National Output) - Long Run

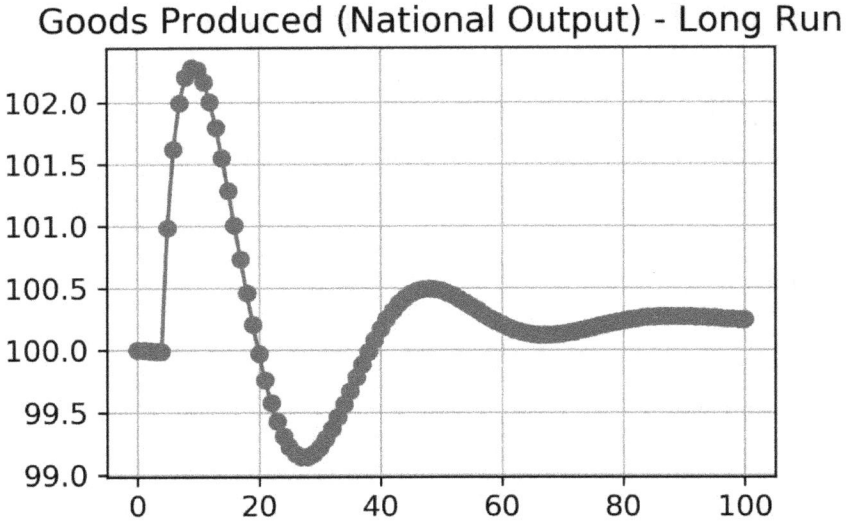

Simulation national output in long run

There are a lot of moving pieces in the model, but the best summary is that investment – both in fixed capital and inventory – overshoot, and then the excess needs to be worked off. Demand from the other sectors is unable to validate the peak investment levels.

Government policy only appears in this model via fiscal policy. Since the economy is not growing in nominal terms in the steady state, the steady state fiscal balance has to be zero (next figure).[47] Once investment picks up in period 5, tax receipts jump while government consumption remains fixed. As a result, the government moves into surplus. In other words, even though fiscal policy settings (the tax rate, spending) are unchanged, the fiscal balance automatically moves to counteract the private sector movements.

---

47   The reasoning is straightforward: in steady state, the debt-to-GDP ratio has to be constant. Since GDP is not growing, it implies debt is not growing. By implication, the fiscal balance must be zero. This is different than an economy growing in nominal terms (which is typical in the real world), as the fiscal deficit must be such that the debt stock is growing in line with nominal GDP.

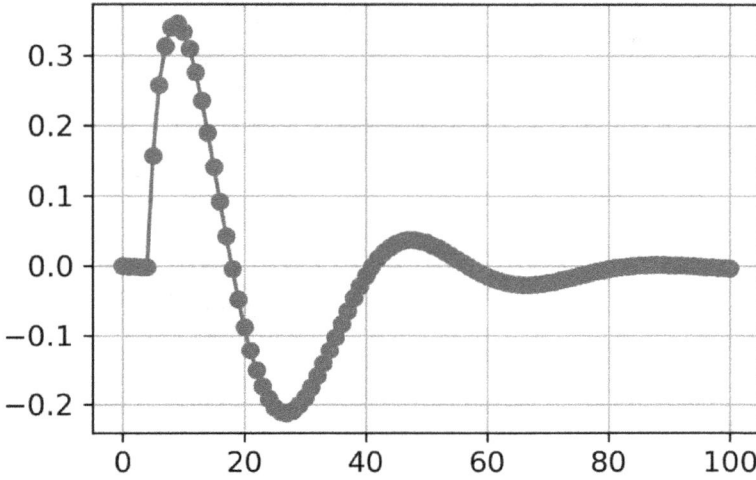

Government Fiscal Balance - Long Run

Simulation fiscal balance in the long run

One small point to note is that the inclusion of private investment slightly increases the steady state multiplier on government consumption. As discussed by Godley and Lavoie in *Monetary Economics*, the level of the output in steady state is a multiple of government consumption. The inclusion of the need for the business sector to replace depreciating capital raises steady state activity. Using the parameter values used in *Monetary Economics* (which this simulation also uses), the multiplier was 5, so government consumption of 20 supported production of 100. In the simulation, the steady state government consumption dropped to 19. The investment model features variable productivity, but the initial steady state was chosen so that the productivity for both models are equal (at 1).

Business Sector (Pro-Forma) Profits

Simulation business sector profits

Although one might think that capital deepening would raise output, the effect was marginal. The explanation appears to be that the model uses a rather neoclassical production function, and so the marginal efficiency of the extra capital is low. The extra depreciation expense due to a higher capital stock reduces steady-state profits in the long run. Since those profits flow through to the household sector via dividends, the lower profits reduce final demand.

(There was a small bump in profits as a result of the initial investment surge. It was surprisingly small, given my reliance on the Kalecki profit equation. I believe the explanation is the somewhat low propensity to consume out of current income for the household sector [0.6] meant that profit increase due to higher investment was largely eaten up by household savings, as well as the move to fiscal surplus.)

Comments on Interpretation

The point that must be underlined is that this model is a stepping-stone to more interesting analysis. By itself, it is a misleading interpretation of the (post-)Keynesian view of business cycles.

This model was my take on Hyman Minsky's interpretation of Keynes, as set out in Minsky's *John Maynard Keynes*. I would point to the passage on page 60:

> *The cyclical succession of system states is not always clearly presented in the "General Theory." In fact, there are two distinct views of the business cycle, one a moderate cycle which can perhaps be identified with a dampened accelerator-multiplier cycle and the second a vigorous "boom and bust" cycle. In chapter 18 (GT, pp. 249-54) Keynes sketches a model of a moderate business cycle that might very well be the prototype for the various nonexplosive accelerator-multiplier interaction models. The business cycle as described is based upon a modest multiplier and a moderately fluctuating prospective yield on investment.*

This model is an SFC implementation of such an accelerator model. We need to dig into the mechanics of how business investment is financed to get models that generate severe booms and busts. Minsky's argument was that Keynes' own explanations of how the financial forms of capitalism generate booms and busts was muddled, which allowed the Old Keynesians to mangle the theory, and revert to the neoclassical synthesis.

To jump ahead to the later logic, the fact that income flows in the real economy multiply the effect of changes of investment leads to the result that investment volatility determines the volatility of overall activity (unless the government manages to do something radically stupid and overwhelm the private sector, such as we saw in the euro periphery under the sage leadership of the neoliberal consensus). That is, if we could predict trends in private investment, we could probably predict the broad trends in growth within a reasonable margin of accuracy. (The sting in the tail is that it is unclear that private investment trends can be easily predicted. If they cannot, then the entire premise of using mathematical models to forecast economic trends is doomed to failure.)

Critiques of SFC Models

I will now turn to some of the various critiques I have seen in the context of SFC models.

- Naïve empiricism. The argument is that we need to pretend to be physicists and immediately fit our models to data. As someone with training in engineering, I would respond that we are facing a complex system, and physicists generally run from complexity and try to isolate underlying principles in simple systems. However, we do not have that luxury when dealing with complex systems. Yes, there are empirical recession models, as I discussed earlier. As I noted, we have no idea what variables we should use for recession forecasting models without having a theory to justify the choices made. We need to ask ourselves: what variables will matter? If we look at a broad class of models that properly account for all income flows – such as this model – we see that those models feature an investment accelerator mechanism. This gives us a strong hint that our empirical research programme should focus on variables related to investment.

- Naïve faith in optimisation. The decision-making rules for the actors in the models are very definitely backwards-looking. Should not the business sector be forward-looking, particularly since investment is literally providing for future activity? There are a number of defects with this argument. The first is that there appears to be little evidence that we could even come up with a tractable optimisation problem if we take into account any uncertainty in the actions of other sectors. The second is that in the real world, firms are not homogeneous, and so even if each individual firm attempts to invest according to some optimal rule, the overall sector behaviour will not be captured by optimising behaviour. The final nail in the coffin is the possibility of irrational behaviour in financial markets; even if firms have an optimal fixed investment plan, the capital markets might not play along.

- Rush to pet models. One common reaction when faced by a mathematical model is for readers to suggest dozens of other mathematical models to look at. There's an infinite number of mathematical models. We should just focus on what useful lessons we can draw from simple ones before we rush off to include every possible theory about economic activity (e.g., what are the banks doing? etc.).

Model Description

We now turn to a fuller description of the model. To those of you who are interested in the equations, they are generated automatically by the model.

Once again, the model is the simplest possible extension of the *sfc_models* framework to allow business sector investment. This was accomplished by taking the simplest (non-trivial) SFC model from *Monetary Economics*, and modifying only the business sector.

If we look at the more advanced SFC models in *Monetary Economics*, there is a well-developed financial system. In the interest of simplicity, there is only a single non-interest bearing financial asset ("money"). This has the side effect of eliminating the issues of capitalist finance, which will be discussed in the next chapter.

Model SIM largely eliminates discussion of the determination of prices; the price of goods is assumed to be fixed, and we only track the nominal income flows in the economy. (Since the price level is fixed, nominal activity is interchangeable with real activity.) The new model largely follows that convention, although wages are now allowed to change, as discussed below. However, these wage changes are largely cosmetic, and so what matters are the nominal income flows.

The household sector receives wage and dividend income, on which it pays tax. (The addition of dividends is new to this model.) It consumes goods (produced by the business sector), with a basic consumption function that is determined by after-tax income and the stock of wealth. There was no attempt to model constraints on the labour force: it was assumed that there was always unemployed labour that could be drawn in by new hiring.

The government sector is the supplier of money and imposes a uniform tax of 20% on household income. (The business sector does not pay tax, which is accidentally realistic.) It also consumes goods produced by the business sector, and this government expenditure is a policy decision that is determined outside the model (an exogenous variable).

In the analysis of model SIM, we see that there is a multiplier from government consumption to overall activity. In the current model, I am keeping government consumption fixed so that we can see the effects of changing trends in investment.

The Business Sector

The changes to the model show up in the business sector. In model SIM, business activity was straightforward: it produced as much goods as was demanded by households and the government, and managed to make no profits when doing so. (The *sfc_models* framework extended this to allow for non-zero profit margins, which entailed the need for dividend payments to recirculate profits back to households.) Production is linearly proportional to labour hired.

The accelerator model adds some complications.

- The business sector no longer knows exactly what demand in the current period will be. It makes a production decision based on the previous period's activity. The implication is that they can make forecast errors for production, and inventories are used as a buffer for forecast misses. (For example, if demand is higher than anticipated, the excess comes from drawing down inventories.)
- Since we assume that decisions in the current period are based only on previously known information, lagged variables are used extensively in business decisions.
- Production now depends on the level of capital (which depreciates). The business sector diverts some goods production to act as gross investment. (Net investment is this gross investment less depreciation.) Since we are fixing the price of goods, one unit of consumption goods is equivalent to one unit of investment goods, and the value of the capital stock is interchangeable with its size in real terms. (There is no market for investment goods that could create a wedge between in the market value of capital and its production cost.) The divergence between the production cost and market value of capital goods is a key part of post-Keynesian theory, which this model unfortunately misses.
- The production function is no longer a linear multiple of hours worked. It is equal to a productivity factor times hours worked, with the productivity factor equal to the square root of the capital stock (measured in real terms) divided by hours worked. This ends up at a very neo-classical looking production function where output is equal to the square root of capital times the square root of hours worked.
- Since productivity changes, keeping wages constant would imply widely varying profit margins – possibly negative. Normal post-Keynesian arguments are that selling prices are set as a mark-up over production costs; in order to keep the model accounting simple, wages are set as a mark-down: wages are set so that businesses keep a constant profit margin (taking into account depreciation costs as well). Rather than track the profit accounting of inventories, the business sector uses a simpli-

fied profit measure that assumes that the cost of goods sold matches the current period's production cost.

- Dividends are paid based on the previous period's profits and cash holdings.

There are two key behavioural conventions followed by the business sector.

- There is a target capital/hours worked ratio. In the initial steady state, this ratio is one. The implication is that the capital stock is equal to the hours worked, and so the variables production, capital and hours worked start out at 100.

- There is a target inventory/sales ratio. (This is a stock-flow norm, as it is a relationship between a stock variable (inventory) and a flow (sales). The value in the simulation is one, so that the target is to hold one period's sales as the stock of inventory.

Both the capital stock and inventory are adjusted slowly towards their target values. The slow adjustment of these variables helps create a relatively low frequency damped business cycle in the model. (Output oscillates, but it tends towards a constant steady state value.)

Concerns About the Model

The model I created is hardly perfect, but it does fit my target of being possibly the simplest possible model. That said, there are a number of issues with it.

- It would have been preferable to take an existing post-Keynesian business cycle model. One issue with that was getting the model to fit within my Python framework. Most post-Keynesian models add a number of complexities that are not yet supported within the framework.

- The behaviour of wages is non-intuitive. A more standard post-Keynesian approach would be to fix wages, then set selling prices as a mark-up. The difference shows up in the initial investment rise in period 5. At that point in time, wages fall when hiring picks up. The reason is straightforward: labour hours rose versus steady state, while capital is still at the steady state value in period 5. Correspondingly, productivity falls, and so the hourly wage drops. If wages were fixed, we would end up with a more sensible-looking inflationary jump in selling prices in response to lower productivity.

- The *sfc_models* framework does not have built-in support of inventory accounting (yet). Rather than build a new accounting system into this model, an approximation for profits is used: prospective profits based on the current cost of production, not the historical cost of production.

- Splitting the household sector into worker and capitalist subsectors would allow for a different propensity to consume out of wages versus dividends. This may allow for a more rapid consumption response to investment increases, under the usual Keynesian argument that households have a higher propensity to consume out of income than out of dividends.

- The addition of an inventory cycle adds an extra source of overshooting. It may be better to have the business sector accurately forecast demand each period (as in model SIM) and eliminate the need for inventories. (This also eliminates the problem of inventory accounting for profit determination.)

Concluding Remarks

This model demonstrates how income flow effects will tend to magnify the effect of changes to fixed investment on overall growth. This allows for moderate business cycles. We need to add financial considerations to the picture to generate greater volatility to the investment cycle. The addition of instability of finance brings us closer to Keynes' description of the cycle.

4.5   Inventory Cycle

Inventories are goods that have been produced but not yet sold to their final customers. The production of goods for inventories is a form of investment, which is a wrinkle to discussions of investment. Like other forms of investment, inventory investment is pro-cyclical: it falls during recessions.

The inventory cycle is typically associated with manufacturers, but it is also a concern for retailers and wholesalers. With the tendency to offshore manufacturing production (and the use of just-in-time inventory management), the argument has been made that the inventory cycle is less significant. Although I have some sympathies for that view, it would require a deeper dive into the pre-1990s data. (I would also note that a survey paper written by Aubik Khan – which will be discussed later – questions that theory.)

The dynamics of inventory investment are slightly different than the dynamics of fixed investment, and we could expect some behavioural differences. Inventory investment is less lumpy than fixed investment, and so somewhat less tied to capital market conditions. That said, a financial crisis will also cut off financing for inventories in much the same way as it would for fixed investment.

Financing Inventories

Inventories are items that a firm expects to be able to sell relatively quickly at a price that is above their cost of acquisition/production. This is unlike fixed assets, which firms do not expect to re-sell at acceptable prices.

The expected fast turnover of inventories means that they are typically matched against short-term financing. This means that sales out of inventories can be used to extinguish the liabilities issued to finance them.

This financing can either be done via financial intermediaries (including commercial paper issuance by larger firms), or via trade finance. This is primarily accounts receivable/payable, although there are specialty lenders that finance things like internationally traded goods.

In economic theory, the natural short-term nature of inventory financing meant that economists argued that this was the main "legitimate" use of bank financing (as in the "real bills doctrine"). This tight linkage between inventories and bank finance shows up in post-Keynesian models, as discussed below.

The short term of inventory financing means that it is somewhat more robust than the financing of fixed investment, which is often done through wholesale markets. (Particularly in the English-speaking world, banks have retreated from financing large-scale fixed investment.) The corporate bond market is somewhat skittish and can often be disrupted for short periods (as a result of a major default, or stock market volatility). The somewhat unreliable nature of the corporate bond market means that competent corporate treasurers do not rely on the bond financing window always being open; they shelve their borrowing plans and wait for animal spirits to return. However, the money markets need to be always open, since entities need to roll their short-term borrowing. Lending standards are supposed to be tighter, borrowers are normally backstopped by bank credit lines, and central banks are always in the background with implicit liquidity support. As a result, the short-term financing market is disrupted less often[48] – but if it is disrupted, the effects are rapidly felt (as in the Financial Crisis).

In other words, inventory investment is unlikely to be affected by typical financial market volatility, unlike fixed investment that is financed by bond issuance. However, if there is a financial crisis that causes a seizure in money markets, the crippling of inventory investment is a rapid-acting channel to the real economy.

Inventory Accounting

Discussions of inventories in the real world end up being clouded by inventory accounting. The reason is that the balance sheet value of inventories can vary widely, depending on the accounting convention. Although these accounting conventions do not matter for the analysis of real goods, they affect reported profits as well as financial ratios. We will now briefly outline how these conventions work. The discussion is based on Chapter 6 of *The Analysis and Use of Financial Statements*, by White, Sondhi, and Fried.[49]

Inventories are goods that are held on the balance sheet; they may either have been produced by the firm or purchased. The value of the inventory units are either the cost of production, or cost to purchase. Typically, the objective is to sell the goods at a profit. If a unit is sold, its value in inventory is referred to as the cost of golds sold and is deducted from the sales price to determine the profit (ignoring other items). Alternatively, the inventory is consumed in the production of goods that are to be sold, and the inventory value of the units is part of the cost of production of the other goods.

Unless the goods are highly differentiated and tracked individually, the inventory is based on the number or volume of goods. In the case of something like crude oil stored in tanks, tracking the goods is

48   The financial press is filled with stories by attention-seeking analysts that cite various jumps in some short-term lending rates. In almost all cases, those jumps in borrowing rates are not economically significant, even for the participants in those markets. After all, there is not a whole lot of price volatility in instruments with a duration close to zero.

49   *The Analysis and Use of Financial Statements, Second Edition*, by Gerald I. White, Ashwinpaul C. Sondhi, Dov Fried, John Wiley & Sons, 1997. ISBN: 0-471-11186-4.

impossible, since different shipments get mixed into the same tank.

Imagine that a firm has 100 units of a good in inventory in the initial year. It produces 100 more units and sells 100 units (keeping the volume of inventory unchanged). This is in an inflationary environment, and so the cost of initial inventory was $50, and the production cost rises by $1 each year.

There are three main inventory accounting methods that may be used.

1. Weighted average cost. In this case, the weighted average cost of units is determined, and then the cost of units sold is based on the average. In the example, the total cost of the 200 units that represent initial inventory is equal to $50×100 + $51×100 = $10,100, which means that the weighted average cost is $50.50. This means that the cost of goods sold is $5,050, and the value of remaining inventory is $5,050. Each year, the cost of goods sold would be averaged up with the cost of production.

2. Last-In, First-Out (LIFO). In this convention, the last goods produced/bought are assumed to be sold first. This means that the average cost of the 100 units sold is equal to the cost of producing them or $51. The value of inventory remains at the old cost: $50. In the next year, the average cost of goods sold rises to $52, while the average value of inventory remains at $50.

3. First-In, First-Out (FIFO). Goods are sold in the order of production. The average cost of goods sold in the first year is equal to the historical inventory cost ($50), while the average cost of inventory units rises to $51. In following years, the average inventory unit cost rises with inflation.

In an inflationary environment, LIFO generates the highest cost of goods sold, and FIFO the least (and weighted average in the middle). This creates a preference for LIFO – since this reduces the profits upon which income taxes are paid. The drawback for LIFO accounting is that inventory values are artificially low, and so they make financial ratios appear less robust.

If a firm is growing, its volume of inventories may always be rising. This means that LIFO inventory values can be based on production costs from much earlier. However, firms may eventually slash their inventories, resulting in a *LIFO liquidation*. The text *The Analysis and Use of Financial Statements* gives examples of LIFO liquidations (page 281) that occurred in 1980-1981 in which firms sold inventory based on production values going as far back as World War II. Given the rise in the price level over that time interval, the cost of goods sold was minuscule relative to their sales price, and so the firms generated abnormally high profits.

From an economic modelling perspective, the weighted average cost method generates the least distortions. Inventories are only slightly lower than market value, while cost of goods sold is relatively close to current production costs, while reflecting some of the holding gains from inflation. Unfortunately, real world data is based on data reported by corporations, and so data needs various adjustments. In a low inflation environment, it is unclear how much these effects matter, but the effect of inflation on accounting figured highly in the discussions of the inflationary era of the 1970s (such as in the writings of Wynne Godey).

The Inventory-Sales Ratio

The inventory-sales ratio is a key analytical tool. Ideally, we want the real inventory-sales ratio: the ratio of the volume of units in inventory divided by the volume of sales in an accounting period. For example, if a car dealer has 200 cars in inventory, and sells 50 per week, the inventory-sales ratio is 4. In practice, we may only have the dollar amounts of inventory, and so the ratio depends on accounting conventions. Since most firms have a mix of goods in inventory, we need to use dollar values to aggregate them.

One point to note is that inventory is a stock variable, while sales is a flow variable. Flow variables are measured with respect to a period of time, and so the inventory-sales ratio depends on the accounting period chosen.

From the perspective of stock-flow consistent modelling, the inventory-sales ratio is tied to the concept of stock-flow norm. Although the difference of units makes direct comparison of stock and flow variables somewhat meaningless, the argument is that actors use ratios between stocks and flows to adjust behaviour. The simplest version is that we assume that a firm wants to keep a certain number of months of sales worth of inventory on hand. Although we can imagine more complex rules being used – particularly for firms with large seasonal variations in demand – one could argue that the effect of these complex rules will be hard to distinguish from a simple rule after we aggregate heterogenous firms.

It is easy to see how having a target inventory-sales ratio causes an accelerator effect. (The investment accelerator model in the previous section includes inventory investment, and there is a small acceleration as a result of it. However, there are more moving parts in that model, so this discussion will look at inventories in isolation.) For simplicity, let us assume that a firm has a target inventory-sales ratio of 1 (i.e., one month's sales), current sales are 100 units, and sales are expected to grow by 1 unit per month.

If the firm starts out with the target inventory-sales ratio, production needs to be 102 units – 101 to meet the expected sales in the next month, plus one unit to grow the inventory to 101 units.

- If actual sales were 102, then sales were equal to production, and the inventory-sales ratio drops to 100/102, and so it is below target. If the firm assumes that the higher-than-expected sales were the result of a permanent increase in demand, expected sales would be 103 in the next month. This implies the need to ramp up production to 106 units: 103 to meet expected demand, plus an extra 3 units to get inventories to 103, so that the inventory-sales ratio is back to 1.
- If actual sales were 99, then 3 more units were produced than sold, and so inventories jump to 103. If the firm extrapolates falling sales, it might only expect to sell 98 units in the next month. This means that production would need to cut production to 93 units – since it needs to liquidate 5 units of inventory that are in excess of the target inventory-sales ratio.

When we look at the data (as discussed below), such an accelerator effect does appear to exist. However, behaviour is likely to be somewhat smoother than that of firms always trying to keep the inventory-sales ratio at a target level. This is achieved in a stock-flow consistent model by having the inventories partially adjust towards their target level. If we use the previous example, this might imply that the firm sets production so that the expected inventory-sales ratio is midway between its current level and the target ratio. That is, if the ratio jumped to 1.1, the target for the next period is 1.05, and production is then set based on expected sales.

The role of expectations is a big theoretical dispute between post-Keynesian and neoclassical economists. However, if one accepts that there might be a target inventory-sales ratio, then the role of expectations is somewhat muted. The only real uncertainty facing firms is the level of future sales. Previous sales forecast mistakes will result in inventories straying from target. At some point, those previous misses will overwhelm the differences between methods to forecast future sales.

A Glance at American Data

The chart below shows the contribution to real GDP growth (annualised basis) from changes in nonfarm inventories, on a quarterly basis.

U.S.: Contribution To Real GDP Growth From Nonfarm Inventories

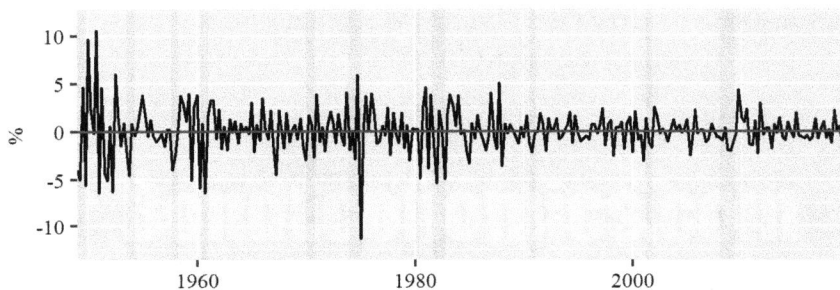

U.S.: Inventory GDP Contribution, 4 Quarter M.A.

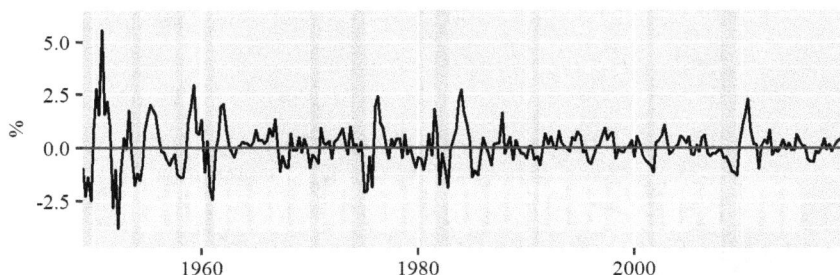

Shade indicates NBER recessions. Source: BEA (via FRED).

U.S. contribution to GDP growth from inventories

The top panel shows the raw contribution to quarterly (annualised) growth, which is quite volatile. (One may note that annualising data magnifies effects, since the quarterly change is effectively multiplied by 4.) This volatility helps ensure that short-term forecasting is challenging. The bottom panel is somewhat more useful, as it smooths out the volatility by plotting the 4-quarter moving average of the above series. As can be seen, there are typically large subtractions from GDP around NBER-designated recessions.

One relatively common argument is that the role of inventories in the business cycle has diminished in recent decades. The movement towards just-in-time inventories has lowered the amount of inventories held, and so there are fewer cyclical swings. If we look at the post-1985 period, this appears relatively plausible – until we hit the 2008 recession, where inventories did result in large swing in real GDP. As a result, we cannot safely say that the inventory cycle has disappeared as a factor; the only real question is whether an inventory correction is enough to trigger a recession.

U.S.: Ratio Of Nonfarm Inventories To Domestic Business Final Sales

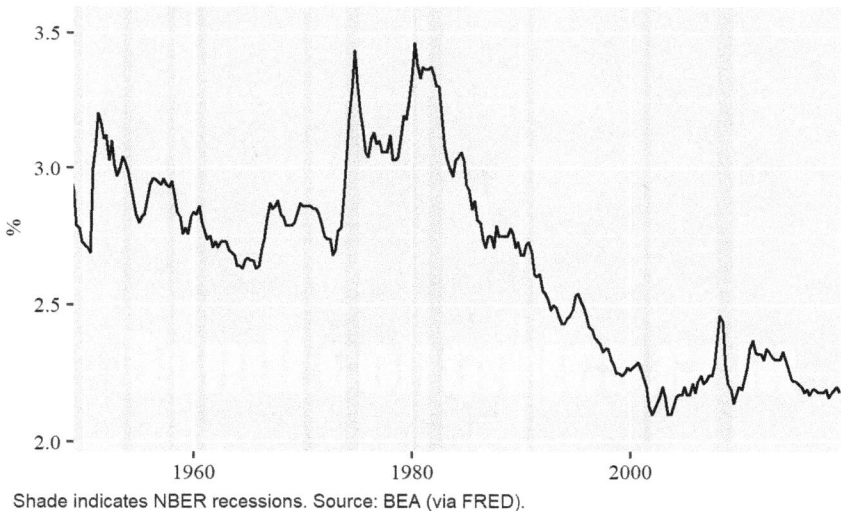

Shade indicates NBER recessions. Source: BEA (via FRED).

U.S. inventory-to-sales ratio

In my view, the main reason to break inventories away from generic "investment" is that it might follow different dynamics than fixed investment. The hope is that we might be able to forecast the cycle based on the trends in inventories. The figure above shows the ratio of aggregated nonfarm inventories to domestic business sales in the United States for the post-war period. Using this measure, the inventory-to-sales ratio has trended lower since the early 1980s, which coincides with the movement towards just-in-time inventories. The ratio spikes in recessions, which reflects falling sales.

Unfortunately for post-Keynesian theory, it is very difficult to detect a target inventory-sales ratio for this measure. For example, it falls steadily from the early 1980s until the 2001 recession. However, the changes in inflation rates and business practices means that I am not too deeply surprised by the lack of a clear target level to which the series reverts.

I am unconvinced that it would be worthwhile pursuing the analysis of aggregated inventories. It seems much more plausible to look at inventories on a per-industry basis. For example, if a sector with normally high inventories shrinks in importance, aggregate inventories would be expected to drop.

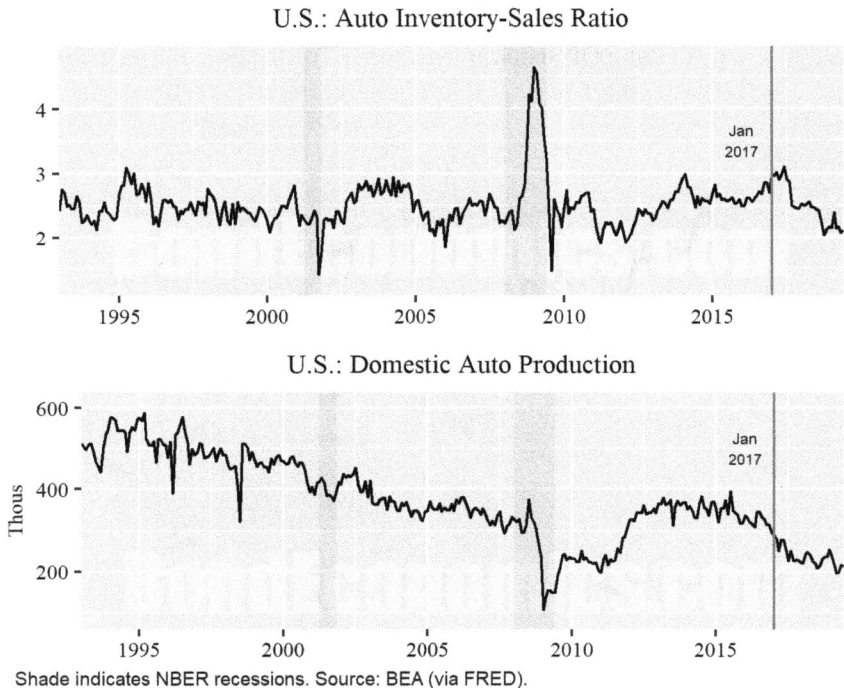

U.S.: Auto Inventory-Sales Ratio

U.S.: Domestic Auto Production

Shade indicates NBER recessions. Source: BEA (via FRED).

U.S. auto inventory-to-sales ratio

The figure above shows the inventory analysis for the U.S. auto sector in the low inflation period starting in 1993 (which is when these monthly series from the Bureau of Economic Analysis start). If we confine ourselves to these data, we have a more plausible basis for arguing in favour that inventory management does follow a stock-flow norm.

The top panel shows the inventory-sales ratio, and it normally sticks between 2 and 3 (months). There are some excursions around recessions, which is to be expected. It is not too hard to come up with a story that production levels (bottom panel) are sensitive to the ratio. For example, take the slowdown in auto production near the end of the data set. The vertical red line marks January 2017, which is where the inventory-sales ratio hit 3 (when rounded). (Note that the date chosen was somewhat arbitrary, but the line was added to create a common time reference on the two panels.) The inventory-sales ratio had been creeping up in 2016, and this was matched by lowered auto production. This was not enough to cause a recession but is one of the contributors to the softness in growth that confounded commentators who expected greater acceleration.

Mainstream Inventory Theories

If we look at standard macro Dynamic Stochastic General Equilibrium models, inventories do not appear. The modelling focus is on expectation formation – particularly in the household sector – and business sector behaviour is stylised. Since the assumption is that products are bought and sold both spot and forward in an optimal fashion, production decisions are just set to give exactly the output needed in the spot market.

Since inventories obviously exist, and are tied to business cycle behaviour, more specialised models have been proposed. My comments here are based on a survey of that literature, "The Role of Inventories in the Business Cycle," by Aubhik Khan.[50] Even so, the argument is that inventory building is a "mystery."

The differences between the mainstream approaches and the post-Keynesian perspective can be summarised as the difference between *randomness* and *uncertainty*. The mainstream approach is based on the assumption that firms are acting in an optimal fashion in the presence of (unknown) random outcomes – that are described by a known probability distribution. The post-Keynesian approach underlines the importance of fundamental uncertainty – we have no idea what the probability distribution is. As a result, decision-making operates in a fog of uncertainty. From a post-Keynesian perspective, holding inventories is no "mystery": firms cannot be certain what will happen in the coming months, so stockpiling key inputs and/or produced goods reduces the risks associated with ad-

50   "The Role of Inventories in the Business Cycle," by Aubik Khan, *Business Review, Federal Reserve Bank of Philadelphia*, 2003, issue Q3, pages 38-45. URL: https://ideas.repec.org/a/fip/fedpbr/y2003iq3p38-45.html

verse outcomes. As a result, even though it is accepted that firms certainly make plans, they are not blindly following the output of some optimisation. The straightforward way to get a grip on inventory management is to survey managers in industries to see what criteria they use to set target inventories. However, one risks drowning in micro data, and so we probably end up backing out simple macro relationships that match observed data in some sense.

Khan's article discusses a few classes of inventory models (as well as giving background on inventory behaviour and the cycle).

- **Production-smoothing.** The model assumes that it is costly to adjust production. Buying new equipment takes time, as would uninstalling unneeded equipment. It takes time to hire and train new employees, while laying them off generates financial costs as well as being bad for morale. The example of toys is given. Christmas sales represent a large chunk of sales, but production levels are normally held steadier to create an inventory to meet the expected surge. The prediction of the model is that production levels should change less than sales. Unfortunately, the model does not really fit the data: observed production is more variable than sales. Another problem is that it is not applicable for input inventories, nor inventory management for intermediary firms (wholesalers, retailers).

- **Increasing Returns to Scale.** Valerie Ramey suggested that increasing returns to scale would result in inventory management behaviour. (Increasing returns to scale imply that production efficiency increases as total output rises.) This model better fits observed data, but also does not apply to non-manufacturers.

- **Random changes to unit costs.** This was a modification proposed by Martin Eichenbaum as a way of increasing the volatility of production to better fit the data. Once again, only applicable to manufacturers.

- **The *(S, s)* model**. The *(S, s)* model was developed by Herbert Scarf, and it suggests that firms face large fixed costs when ordering or producing goods. This implies that firms are biased to have large orders infrequently. This creates the needed volatility in production to match the data. Furthermore, the model can be adapted to non-manufacturing firms.

These mainstream models will be attractive to many people, as they provide mathematical models that can be fit to data, and they offer some predictive value. However, the post-Keynesian critique is straightforward: we ought to survey firms and see how they set their target inventory levels. Since different industries will have different preoccupations, it is extremely likely that reality is far more complex than these models suggest. To the extent that the mainstream models work, it is just the reality that we can match almost any plausible simplified model to observed data. This is a debate that is removed from the question of inventory recessions (since both neoclassical models and post-Keynesian models can generate an inventory accumulation cycle), and so there is no value in pursuing the topic herein.

Adding Information, But…

I would put forth the example of auto inventories as a case where we can use the inventory-sales ratio as a predictive variable on a per-industry basis. In principle, that might be enough to predict an inventory-led recession. If one wanted to come up with methodologies to back-cast historical recessions, that might be a possible angle of attack.

That said, the value of that approach is much less clear in the post-1990 era. Even if one can forecast a slowdown in production in particular industries using inventory data, it might not be enough (other than for regional recessions). Manufacturing is a shrinking component of overall employment, and the reality is that firms can trim production without layoffs. Although there are presumably "multiplier effects" from a firm cutting overtime hours, these will presumably be less disruptive than laying off workers.

Correspondingly, inventory analysis is going to be useful in attempts to build "bottom up" growth forecasts, where forecasts are made on a per-sector basis. The concern with such approaches is that they end up being extremely sensitive to the choices made in how to stitch partial models together. The risk is that one ends up with a final forecast that is entirely tuned to the biases of the people running the model.

Finally, I am currently agnostic on the question of whether changes in inventory management explain the lower frequency of recessions in recent decades. I expect to return to empirical analysis of competing theories in the second volume. Given the large number of structural changes to the economy, as well as policymaker behaviour since the early 1980s, I am not hopeful that I can disentangle the effects of inventory management changes on their own. Moreover, we cannot say that the inventory cycle has been abolished – it certainly helped magnify the contraction of the economy after the Financial Crisis.

4.6   The Household Sector and Recessions

Thus far, the focus has been on the tendency for the business sector to generate a cycle in growth. Household behaviour was assumed to be stable, to allow us to examine the feedback loops created by investment. We now examine the effects of changing household behaviour. To a certain extent, changes in household behaviour has been a major driver of the post-1990 business cycle in the developed countries. In particular, the housing market has become a dominant economic force (which will be discussed at greater length in the second volume in its own dedicated chapter).

The first point to note is that we need to look beyond one obvious point: a drop in household consumption will typically represent a large percentage of the reduction of GDP during a recession. Household consumption is a large percentage of total expenditures in the economy, and it would be quite difficult for GDP to contract when household consumption is rising. We are assuming one stylised fact: that consumption is a large percentage of income for households. If we use a stronger definition of recession than just a decline in GDP (for example, the NBER definition), a recession implies an increase in unemployment. It is not particularly surprising that people who lose their job spend less.

Instead, we need to look at three types of behavioural shifts that could be linked to the start of a recession (not in order of importance).

1.   Households could change consumption patterns in a way that lowers domestic output.
2.   Investment tied to households could increase.
3.   Households could reduce spending relative to incomes (or wealth): the propensity to consume.

Changing Consumption Patterns

The first possibility – a change in consumption patterns – is somewhat difficult to model at the macro level. The only plausible example I can give is a repeat of the oil shock, where the price of energy soars. If the energy is imported, spending will be diverted to imports, which is a drag on GDP and profits. In addition, even if the energy is produced domestically, the energy sector will not be able to increase employment rapidly enough to offset losses in other sectors. However, in the case of an energy shock, all sectors will be affected, not just households. (Oil shocks are returned to in Section 4.7.)

Household Investment

The second possibility – changes in investment associated with the household sector – is important, but somewhat of a misnomer. Depending on the definitions used in the national accounts, very little investment may be associated with the household sector currently. This would not always have to be the case. For example, one could imagine the rise of consulting-style businesses that results in "business" investment activity being measured as part of household expenditures. (The driver of this switch could be technology or tax arbitrage.) However, I would argue that this theoretical possibility is really a measurement issue: from a theoretical perspective, the behaviour should be lumped in with the modelled business sector.

The main investment associated with the household sector is residential investment, and if we want to be loose with our definitions, the housing market more generally. Although the purchase of an existing house does not qualify as "investment:" in the national accounts sense (as it is just a transfer of an existing asset), it is an "investment" in the other sense of the word: a portfolio allocation transaction. Residential investment may be classified under business sector investment, but it is really tied to household sector activity, so it should really be analysed separately. However, as noted earlier, the discussion of the housing market is put aside until the second volume. The remainder of this section puts housing market issues to the side.

The only remaining "investment" that might be associated with the household sector would be the purchase of durable goods. From a national accounts perspective, these expenditures are typically classified as current consumption. However, we might want to break out important categories, most notably vehicles. The automobile industry is cyclical, and demand is sensitive to the existing stock of vehicles. From a modelling perspective, the interesting part of durable goods expenditures is that they should be more interest rate sensitive than other expenditures. Auto loans and leases are far more common than loans for iced coffee drinks. This should show up in models that analyse the effects of interest rates on household consumption (as in the neoclassical models in the second volume).

Changing Propensity to Consume

We are left with the possibility of a change in the propensity to consume. Broadly, neoclassical models are more likely to associate business cycle fluctuations to changes in the propensity to consume. The post-Keynesian bias is to treat consumption patterns as being more stable, but with a much greater emphasis on the effects of the distribution of income. The argument is that lower income households (workers) have a greater propensity to consume out of current income than high income households (capitalists), and so a change in the distribution of income will change the aggregate propensity to consume. The neoclassical literature does its best to avoid questions of the distribution of income, with this tendency reaching its apex in the "representative household" class of models.

It is clear that a drop in household consumption will have an immediate impact on growth, as inventories will pile up and/or business sector profits will fall. This would trigger a retrenchment in production, which will then recirculate because of falling wage incomes as hours are cut.

The notion of a "tendency to consume" is vague. Within SFC models, there are typically two propensities to consume: what percentage of current income is consumed, and (loosely speaking) what percentage of wealth is consumed. (Most people do not consume things like bearer bonds, yet they affect the consumption function, and wealth is adjusted via the budget equation.) Depending on the model, we could have different propensities for different categories of income or wealth. One typical division would be to differentiate consumption out of dividends versus wage income, which is one way to attempt to capture the different propensities to consume for different income/wealth quantiles.

One problem is that we can only observe a single, aggregated level of consumption, and aggregated income statistics. (Information on income distributions typically arrives with a long lag and is often only annual in frequency.) If we allow time-varying propensities to consume (which is the premise here), we may not be able to fit all the parameters to the available data. As such, we would need to be careful how we compare model results to observed data.

Modelled Consumption Shock

We will now examine a simplified model, which is the basic investment accelerator model of Section 4.4. Instead of applying a shock to the investment parameter, we apply a shock to the propensity to consume out of income. The simulation results below were generated by the script *ex20190324_consumption_propensity.py* which is included in the source code of the *sfc_models* package.

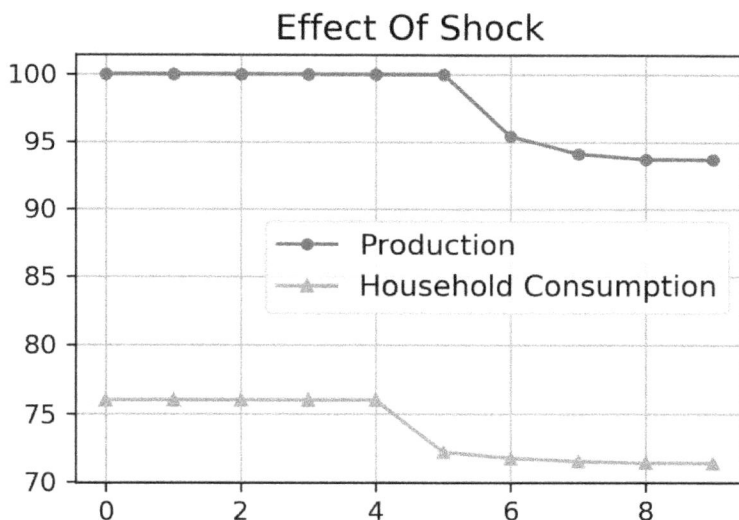

Simulated consumption shock

The above figure depicts the time series for household consumption and total production if the propensity to consume out of income drops from 0.6 to 0.55 in period 5 (and remains there). (The parameter value of 0.6 is the value used by Godley and Lavoie in model SIM in the textbook *Monetary Economics*.) The key point to note is that consumption immediately falls in period 5, while production falls in period 6. Since the production function is based on work hours and capital, work hours (not shown) would only fall in period 6. This is because the business sector sets work hours "in advance" of the time period and is assumed to not be able to adjust work hours immediately in response to lower demand. This is not a property of all models; many SFC and DSGE models will have goods market clearing that forces work hours to adjust simultaneously. Post-Keynesians normally object to such a market clearing assumption, but it could be justified if the time period is sufficiently long. (The simplest SFC models in *Monetary Economics* feature such market clearing.) Since we need to have a relatively fine time step (most likely monthly) to capture the short-lived nature of most recessions, having businesses unable to react to the current period demand seems plausible.

Inventory

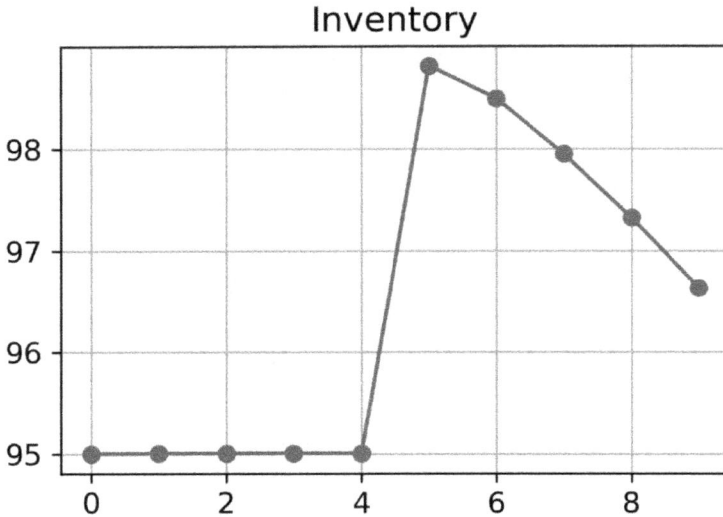

Simulation inventory

The drop in consumption has a multiplier effect within the model. The figure above depicts the level of inventories. They immediately jump in period 5, which is a necessary consequence of the business sector reacting with a lag to changes in demand. Since sales were less than forecast, unsold goods pile up in inventory. The inventory level then drops in subsequent periods. This is because businesses cut production to return the inventory/sales ratio to its target (which is 1 in the model). Cutting inventories is a form of disinvestment, and explains the drop in production in period 6.

Gross Investment

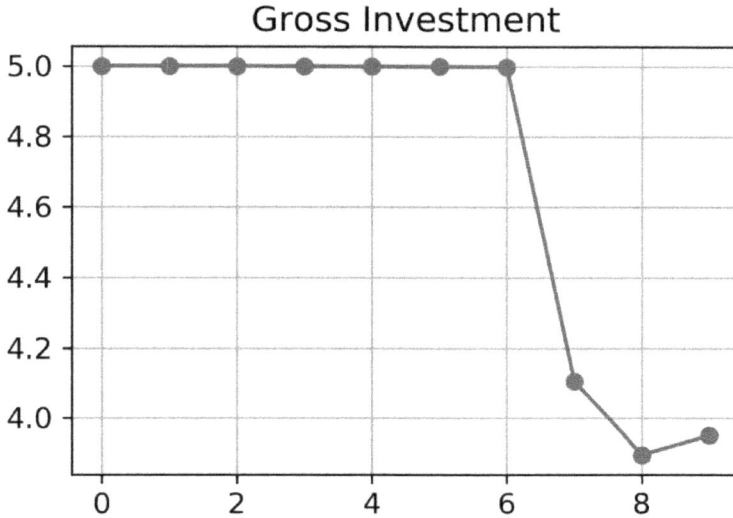

Simulation investment

The dropping production lowers the target level of capital, and we see that fixed investment starts to fall in period 7. This is another way in which the change in the propensity to consume has a multiplier effect on total output. The key point to note is that the change in investment occurs two time periods after the change in consumption.

This tells us what to look for if we want to believe that consumption propensity changes cause recessions: consumption needs to fall ahead of the downturn in activity. The simple way to do this is to examine the appropriate time series, or one could try to appeal to various statistical tests.

Limited Use for Forecasts

The model demonstrated earlier does not offer a good starting point for recession forecasting. The issue is that the model offers almost no useful information for recession forecasting if we believe that the propensity to consume is an exogenous parameter. Since we have no reason to believe that we can forecast exogenous parameter value changes, such an analysis suggests that recessions just happen. We will only get some more useful information if we argue that the propensity to consume is a function of some measurable variables, such as the rate of interest.

If we extended the model, we might be able to generate more useful information. One possible enhancement would be to break out durable goods (e.g., autos), as discussed earlier. The other would be to take into account financial disruptions to consumption.

Wealth Effect

Finally, we could look at the propensity to consume out of wealth. If we take the previous investment accelerator model, a change to the propensity to consume out of wealth would be nearly impossible to distinguish from the propensity to consume out of income. The reason for this is that the only household wealth in the model that appears in the consumption function is money holdings. (Equity ownership is implied by dividends, but the value of equity does not appear in the consumption function.) More complex SFC models include a range of financial assets. If the subject of interest were economic expansions, the so-called "wealth effect" is of greater interest. The wealth effect was a subject of interest in the 1990s. For example, what was the effect of the ongoing twin bull markets in stocks and house prices on the economy? However, the wealth effect was assumed to be too slow-moving, and it would be hard to tie to recessions. Household wealth levels would only change quickly in the context of some form of crisis in asset markets (e.g., stock market crash), and whatever caused that market crisis would presumably be tied to rising recession risks.

Summary

The housing market is the most obvious channel by which household sector behaviour on its own can trigger a recession and will be discussed in the next volume. Otherwise, if one wants a theory that potentially generates useful predictions, one either moves to the topic of disruptions within the financial markets, or the possibility that the propensity to consume is a function of interest rates. Those topics will be discussed in later chapters.

4.7 The External Sector and Recessions

If we look at countries with some form of a currency peg system, or developing countries, there are numerous recessions, crises, and depressions associated with shocks from the *external sector* (interactions with the rest of the world).

From the perspective of my arguments about the ability to forecast recessions, such external crises do not appear to be an exception. Although nobody is going to be surprised by the default of certain countries, the question of timing is paramount in order to be able to claim to forecast the crisis. It is certainly possible to imagine that analysts can convert the information in some economic and financial time series into indicators that offer a probability distribution for the odds of a crisis. My argument is that although such an indicator is a mathematical model in a broad sense, it is not an attempt to simulate the economy. Such indicators may have their uses, but they are vulnerable to changing definitions to input series and cannot be used to model the effects of policy changes. That is, they are mathematical models, but not *macroeconomic* models, which is the subject of my discussion.

Most of the discussion of external crises will revolve around financial aspects of the crisis, such as a collapsing currency. Those financial aspects of external crises are discussed in Section 5.5. This section focuses on the mechanisms within the real economy that will transmit pressures from the external sector towards recession risks. These possible transmission mechanisms are covered in turn.

Strengthening Currency

Although the popular imagination is drawn to currency collapse scenarios, it is possible that currency strengthening can be more easily associated with recessions for floating currency sovereigns.

The argument as to why a strengthening currency will cause a recession is straightforward: a country whose currency appreciates faces a loss of international competitiveness with respect to exports. This is because domestic labour costs are an important component of production costs, and wages in the developed countries are not indexed to the value of the currency. That is, the cost of production in a foreign currency will rise. Unless the country sells products for which this production cost increase does not matter, the country is expected to lose market share.

I have some sympathy for this view, and we can use it to discuss some historical episodes. However, there is an immediate problem with it: if we fix our period of interest as 1995-2018, we see that recessions in most developed countries were largely synchronised: there was the technology bubble bursting in 2000-2001, and the Financial Crisis.[51] Not every devel-

51   If we look at business cycles before 1995, there was greater decorrelation. For example, Japan had an investment boon-bust cycle that was not correlated with other countries. European economies had diverging

oped country had recessions during those episodes, but most faced slow-downs. The problem is straightforward: since currency movements are relative price shifts, to a certain extent, foreign exchange movements should have the opposite effects on trading partners. If the business cycle remains synchronised, this means that the currency movement cannot have been the determining factor.

Weakening Currency

By itself, a currency weakening makes a country's exporters relatively more competitive, since domestic wages will fall relative to global wages. Imported input costs rise in domestic currency terms but those prices are the same as those faced by international competitors. This improvement of competitiveness should tend to improve the prospects for investment, and thus raise output. For the fall in the currency to cause weaker growth, other factors will need to kick in.

The most important factor would be a financial crisis. The most likely form of crisis is the expectation of major defaults by either the sovereign, banks, or large industrial firms. The panic selling of domestic financial assets in order to invest in safer securities elsewhere drives down the currency. One can point to many such episodes in history. Since this is really a story about financial crises, I will defer its discussion to Section 5.5.

If we put aside the possibility of a financial crisis, there are two plausible mechanisms for a recession. The first is that a falling currency raises the inflation rate, triggering a policy-induced recession. The second mechanism is an effect like historical oil price shocks.

The mainstream consensus view was that the costs of inflation are high, and it is the job of central banks to control inflation. A weakening currency will tend to raise the price of imports, which can feed into the domestic inflation process. (Like many others, I am skeptical about the strength of this effect at present in most developed countries but will put that aside for now.) In order to keep the inflation process under control, many central banks will raise interest rates in an attempt to defend the value of the currency. These rapid interest rate rises could induce a recession.

One historic example was the Bank of England raising rates to defend the pound's level within the Exchange Rate Mechanism in 1992. Given fortunes as a result of German reunification, and the breakup of the Exchange Rate Mechanism.

that the United Kingdom had an over-extended housing market, the rise in interest rates led to a downturn. Of course, one may note that was a fixed exchange rate system; examples involving floating rate systems are less obvious.

Oil Shocks

Another plausible mechanism to generate a recession is that the rise in the price of imported necessities will reduce the demand for domestically produced goods. The most important example is the various oil shocks that have occurred since the 1970s. Although oil shocks were the historical experience, one could imagine massive simultaneous crop failures causing similar problems. Oil price spikes are somewhat distinct from most discussions of the "external sector" as the price of oil was rising relative to all currencies, so this is not related to the usual concern of a single country facing adverse circumstances with trade.

West Texas Intermediate Crude Price Changes And U.S. Recessions

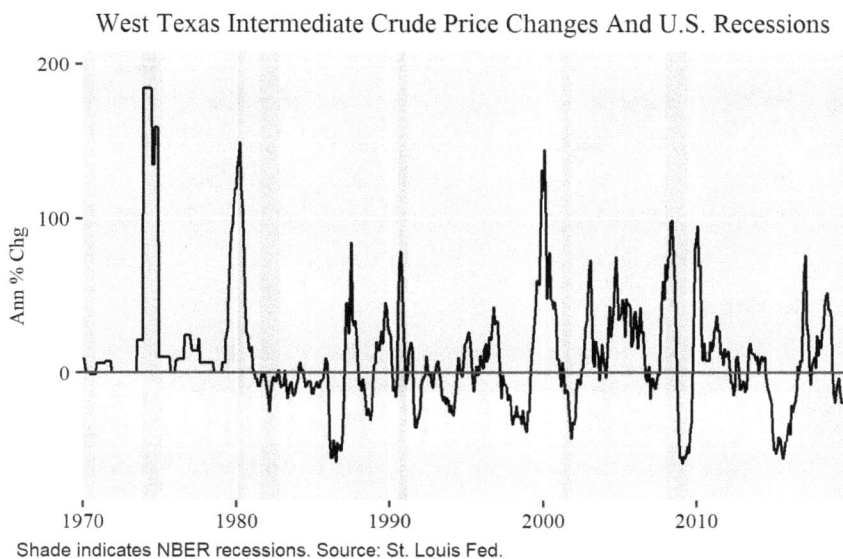

Shade indicates NBER recessions. Source: St. Louis Fed.

West Texas Intermediate crude oil price and recessions

The fact that oil price spikes have preceded U.S. recessions since the early 1970s (figure above) is heavily cited in discussing the importance of energy prices in creating recessionary conditions. (The streak was broken in 2020, so this relationship might be cited less going forward.) The argument is straightforward: industrial societies are heavily dependent upon hydrocarbon energy sources, so a spike in energy prices has a depressing effect on economic activity. There are a few channels for this effect. The first is the redirection of income flows towards oil exporters (and most developed countries are oil importers), which is why I lump oil price spikes with external sector sources of recession. The next problem energy price spikes pose is that the rise in energy costs for consumers means that they redirect spending, implying that other sectors of the economy will face falling revenues, and thus risk bankruptcy and/or staff layoffs. Finally, the uncertainty about oil price spikes (and falling revenue) will depress investment in industries that do not benefit from higher energy prices.

There is no doubt that an energy price spike will be a negative for growth. There are two ways of generating such a spike in a country: oil prices rise versus all currencies, or the currency of the country collapses. The cost of "strategic imports" is probably the main reason to fear a currency collapse (the other main concern being food prices).

Nevertheless, I would not lean too heavily on the "oil price spikes cause recessions" theory, which was popular in Peak Oil circles. Not all countries are oil importers – an oil exporter welcomes the higher price. Not all countries have the same recessionary periods as the United States, even though oil prices were spiking in all major currencies at the same time. Even for the United States, the recessions since 1990 coincided with problems in the financial sector that would have derailed the economy anyway.

Trade Policy

The final possible mechanism for a recession due to the external sector is a policy-driven disruption in trade, without reference to what is happening to the value of the currency. This could be either the result of tit-for-tat protectionist policies being enacted (as has been the case in 2019 between the United States and other countries), or the breakdown of a trade agreement (such as the exit of the United Kingdom from the European Union, which is currently underway at the time of writing). Furthermore, one could point to geopolitical concerns, such as a trade embargo or major war.

Since these previously cited situations are developing at the time of writing, I will largely not attempt to guess what the outcomes will be. Otherwise, we do not have too many examples of such trade frictions in the modern era. (Tariffs were part of the backdrop of the Great Depression.)

There is no doubt that disruptions to trade can cause a recession. Cutting off key inputs to manufacturing or the loss of export markets will force industries to cut production. This presumably will have a knock-on effect on investment, and so the investment-accelerator effect will kick in.

It is unclear how easy it is to model such effects from a macro perspective. For example, industrial users losing access to natural gas supplies might cripple production. Conversely, a tariff on playing cards (which Canada enacted as part of trade "negotiations" with the United States) may be annoying for trading card game players, but it is entirely likely that their discretionary spending would be diverted to alternative leisure activities, and so there may be almost no effect on the domestic economy. We would need to somehow model the sectoral effects of the policy change, and it is unclear whether we would have much data to calibrate the parameters used. We would be stuck with making judgement calls about the effects, which is essentially a way of getting a model to reproduce whatever we want it to say. Of course, one can have good judgement, but one would need to be very cautious about any claims of empirical backing to the results.

From the forecasting perspective, this appears to be a variant of policy-induced recessions. An extreme policy change could easily be associated with high recession odds. As such, a recession is forecastable. Nevertheless, this once again turns into a political analysis, and is not a pure econometric exercise.

Summary

In my view, the role of the external sector in recessions revolves mainly around the possibility of a financial crisis. This will be returned to in Section 5.5. Otherwise, we would need to relate external developments to what is happening in the real economy, and we need to do very delicate sectoral analyses. The possibility of drastic policy changes causing a recession is always there, but this is a question of political analysis as to whether such changes will be made.

4.8 Animal Spirits and Fixed Investment

The previous sections of this chapter offered straightforward observations about the economy and were not closely tied to post-Keynesian theory. Once we turn to the concept of animal spirits, the linkage to the post-Keynesian literature is clearer. Since profits and growth are tied to fixed investment, the determination of fixed investment trends is critical for recession analysis. Instead of appealing to optimising behaviour, post-Keynesians argue that uncertainty clouds the outlook for decision-makers. A recession can be triggered by shifting optimism about the future.

Since the discussion of financial considerations is deferred to the next chapter, the discussion here is somewhat generic. There are a few competing approaches to the determination of investment within the post-Keynesian literature, but the differences are relatively minor if we want to focus on recessions. This discussion is essentially based on the survey found in Chapter 6 of Marc Lavoie's *Post-Keynesian Economics: New Foundations*.[52]

Propensities to Invest

The post-Keynesian models of interest modelled the rate of investment in terms of a few factors, one of which is a constant denoted γ (Greek lowercase gamma), which is an exogenous parameter. Other terms within the investment equation varied depending on the model, but they consisted of a propensity to invest (gamma with an appropriate subscript) multiplying another variable. On page 349, Lavoie states that the gamma parameters "reflect the intensity of the animal spirits of the entrepreneurs." To provide some examples of the variables that are used, Steindl included the retention ratio, the debt leverage ratio, the rate of profit, and capacity utilisation rate (as seen on page 361 of *Post-Keynesian Economics*).

In an expansion, the mix of terms in the investment equation would be of great empirical interest. For example, what factors offer the most explanatory power over time? For our purposes here, all that we are interested in is isolating the cause of a rapid downturn in investment.

Until the recession has been underway, the fundamental variables in the investment equation will not have shifted for most firms. (Some sectors will have started contracting ahead of the recession, and so their fundamentals will have deteriorated.) However, beliefs about the future can shift much more quickly than the accounting data. Although models may use historical values for the fundamental inputs to the investment equation, we know that is only a proxy for what matters: expectations for the future. The forecast values for capacity utilisation, etc. would likely be downgrad-

52 *Post-Keynesian Economics: New Foundations*, by Marc Lavoie 2014. Edward Elgar, 2014. ISBN: 978-1-78347-582-7.

ed if there were a panic regarding future growth prospects. Since we do have access to those forecasts, if we tried to fit the model to observed data, it would appear that the gamma multipliers fell rapidly, since the accounting data will not yet have moved.

Animal Spirits

Things get worse if there are nonlinearities present in the thought process behind investment. If we imagined that businesses transitioned from a risk-seeking state to a risk-averse state based on some non-measurable "animal spirits" variable, we could have a step change in investment if "animal spirits" crossed some threshold. (Think of the animal spirits as being the hidden variable in a Markov switching model, like the models discussed in Section 2.2.) Since such events are rare (recessions are now about a decade apart), we could not really hope to gather enough information to be able to forecast the transitions of this hidden variable.

If we believe that the real world resembled a model with that structure, it is extremely awkward for recession forecasting. Since we cannot measure the "animal spirits" variable, we cannot hope to pin down when a recession would start. We only see the effect of the state change by the rapid deterioration in activity variables – that is, after the recession has essentially started.

We might hope to use measured variables as a proxy for such a variable; in my view, explains why the stock market sort-of works as a recession indicator. (The problem is the number of false positives.)

Nevertheless, it is unclear how much we can attribute "animal spirits" to purely real factors alone. The financial sector is somewhat centralised, and its tendency to withdraw credit in a systemic fashion is perhaps more important for modern business cycles. That is the subject of Chapter 5.

As a final note, even though financial factors matter for recessions, the factors noted here are still rooted in the real economy. Although the Financial Crisis has spawned many calls for radical reform of the banking system, I doubt that this would be enough to abolish the cycle. Fixed investment is pro-cyclical, almost by definition. As will be discussed in the second volume, the housing market is a key source of fixed investment – and it is a market, with all the possibilities for booms and busts.

Chapter 5 Heterodox Financial Business Cycle Theory

5.1   Introduction

Although a retrenchment in fixed investment solely due to changes in animal spirits within the real economy is possible, this is not necessarily the most likely cause of a recession. In recent decades, the financial sector has been hyperactive, and tends to augment the instability of the real economy.

The instability of capitalist finance has been heavily discussed in the aftermath of the Financial Crisis. In this chapter, Hyman Minsky's Financial Instability Hypothesis is discussed at length. Minsky's work provides the most distinctive post-Keynesian theory of recessions.

The Financial Instability Hypothesis suggests that there is what is known as a "super-cycle": structural changes in behaviour that persist across multiple business cycles, and then reverse. This differs from conventional theories that suggest that economic behavioural parameters are relatively stable over time.

The importance of financing investment means that we cannot abstract away the financial sector from economic models, which is a standard complaint against neoclassical models that was levelled by heterodox authors both before and after the Financial Crisis. (To be fair to the neoclassicals, finance was not ignored in all of their models, and it is certainly a topic of research post-crisis. I will defer discussion of those models until the second volume.)

This chapter is labelled "*Heterodox* Financial Business Cycle Theory" and not "Post-Keynesian" since there is a section on Austrian economics. I am not a fan of Austrian economic theory, but I would argue that many Austrian commentators develop business cycle stories that share some characteristics of post-Keynesian ones. From an academic perspective, there is a very large divide between post-Keynesian and Austrian economics. However, if one reads financial market commentary produced by self-described Austrians, we can see some overlap in thinking about the mechanisms behind recessions.

5.2   Financial Instability Hypothesis – Borrowers

The *Financial Instability Hypothesis* was associated with the economist Hyman Minsky, although it can be viewed as Minsky's interpretation of Keynes. One summary of the concept is that stability is destabilising: economic stability leads to changes in behavioural changes that destabilise the economy.

The Financial Instability Hypothesis is complex, and so I am splitting the concept into two parts. The first part is a discussion of the evolution of the behaviour of borrowers. The second is the evolution of the financial system, a discussion that will be deferred to Section 5.3. Although these two dynamics are linked, it is simpler to discuss them separately.

Minsky and Multiplier Models

My discussion here leans heavily on Chapter 3 of the book *Why Minsky Matters: An Introduction to the Work of a Maverick Economist* by L. Randall Wray.[53] If one wants to read Minsky's original text, the book *Can "It" Happen Again? Essays on Instability and Finance*[54] has multiple essays on the subject.

Although Minsky studied at Harvard, he rejected the simplified IS/LM model that was the Harvard approach of the time, instead he preferred the multiplier-accelerator model developed by fellow student Paul Samuelson. However, as L. Randall Wray notes:

> *Whereas that model [the accelerator model] at least allowed for instability, the problem was that it was too unstable: gross domestic product (GDP) could shoot off toward infinity or toward zero, depending on assumptions.*

I was not completely satisfied with the formal models used by Minsky, for reasons such as the above. My preference is to use a stock-flow consistent (SFC) model that will generate the investment multiplier effect, as done in Section 4.4. Since the modelling technique used is a hybrid based on the work of a number of heterodox authors, a historian of economic thought could argue that my presentation is not purely Minsky's theo-

---

53   *Why Minsky Matters: An Introduction to the Work of a Maverick Economist* by L. Randall Wray, Princeton University Press, 2016. ISBN: 978-0-691-15912-6.

54   *Can "It" Happen Again? Essays on Instability and Finance,* by Hyman P. Minsky, M.E. Sharpe, Inc., 1984. ISBN: 0-87332-213-4.

ry.[55] In any event, Minsky viewed his work as an interpretation of Keynes (that Keynes was not able to make clear before his death), and his theory evolved as he incorporated other post-Keynesian concepts (such as the Kalecki profit equation).

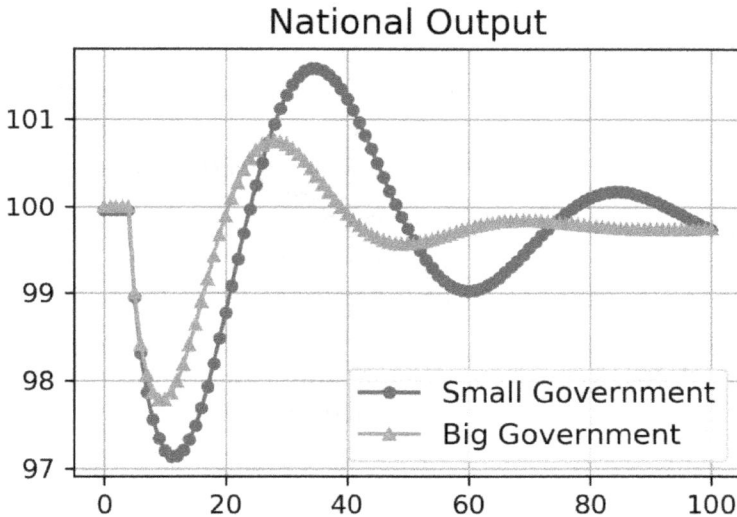

National Output

Simulated national output with small and large governments

The use of more modern modelling techniques has one side effect – it buries the question of why the economy is stable. When one argues that capitalism is inherently unstable, we need to be able to explain why growth is in fact relatively steady during an expansion. The SFC accelerator model of Section 4.4 was naturally stable – because of the automatic stabiliser provided by the government. (More complex SFC models will include other factors that will also stabilise activity.) The figure above shows two simulations of a shock generated by a reduction in the propensity to invest.[56] The only difference in parameter values is that the "small government" is

---

55   My accelerator model would even be more problematic as I used some neoclassical-looking modelling choices as shortcuts to simplify price determination.

56   The code to generate this example is found at https://github.com/brianr747/SFC_models/blob/master/sfc_models/examples/scripts/ex201904110_accelerator_gummint.py

half the size of the "big government" (tax rate is 10% instead of 20%, and government consumption is 9.5 instead of 19). The reduction in the size of the government sector means that it has less of an automatic stabilisation effect. (Since tax rates and government consumption are constant – and there is no monetary policy – the stabilisation is entirely automatic.) This illustrates Minsky's argument that "Big Government" and the "Big Bank" (the Federal Reserve) "constrained instability, particularly downside risks" (quotation from Wray). These institutional changes explained why depressions generally did not happen in developed countries in the post-World War II era (the post-Financial Crisis euro periphery being an exception).[57]

Hedge/Speculative/Ponzi Borrowers

Having covered the explanation as to why the economy is sort-of stable, we can then turn to the source of instability that Minsky identified. This is the famous hedge-speculative-Ponzi borrower spectrum that he defined.

- A *hedge borrower* borrows in such a fashion that expected cash flows would cover all required payment flows from borrowing. Currently, the best example of such borrowers would be households that have long-dated amortising mortgages that should be extinguished under the assumption of continued employment.

- A s*peculative borrower* is a borrower that has debt repayment flows that are not covered by immediate cash flows but could be covered by later cash flows if the borrower has access to capital markets and can roll over the debt. Technically, the net present value of income flows are larger than the net present value of debt flows, the issue is only of timing. This is referred to as speculative since the borrowing is operating on the premise that lenders in the future will be open to offering new financing in order to roll over debt. In practice, modern corporations would tend to be classified as speculative borrowers, other than some with extremely clean balance sheets. (There might be exceptions, such as infrastructure projects that operate on a cash flow matched basis.)

- A *Ponzi borrower* (named after the early financial engineer, Charles Ponzi) is a borrower that has a net present value of cash

57   I would like to thank Twitter user @bluser12 for pointing out that a draft version of this sentence was mangled.

flow that is less than the net present value of expected income. Unless the borrowing is done on a fraudulent basis (which can happen), this only makes sense if there is an expectation of rising asset prices, rising income from the assets, or falling interest rates. My feeling is that the normal practice would be to bury these optimistic assumptions into expected value, and so the borrower would be classified as speculative. However, if one extrapolates current income forward, we would end up with borrowers slipping from speculative to Ponzi because extrapolated current income is below actual expectations.

As my description suggests, most corporate borrowing would fall in the speculative category if we looked at the cash flow estimates used by borrowers and lenders. Sub-prime residential lending in the United States before the Financial Crisis acts as a real-world example of Ponzi borrowing. The premise behind the more plausible versions of these loans (some categories of sub-prime lending made no sense) was that the borrower had a bad credit rating that could be improved after demonstrating a history of meeting the mortgage payments. After a few years, the improvement in the credit rating would allow a refinancing into a conventional mortgage at a lower interest rate, converting the form of finance to hedge financing. Meanwhile, the lender was supposed to be protected by the assumed rise in house prices in aggregate (since lenders had portfolios that were diversified geographically). That lending strategy worked – until it didn't.

Financial Instability Hypothesis

Once this categorisation is set, we then return to the Financial Instability Hypothesis. Minsky's argument was that lending and borrowing standards are set by conventions, and those conventions vary over time. Assume that we start out with very cautious lenders and borrowers (which was the case after the Great Depression and World War II). The bulk of borrowers fall into the hedge category or are possibly speculative. However, assume that the economy grows steadily, and businesses are generally successful. The firms that use more leverage will end up with a higher rate of return on assets and they would repay their loans. All agents will revise their views about borrowing conventions and decide that the standards met by the relatively higher risk borrowers were adequately safe. Therefore, standards are loosened progressively.

This is not just an issue of psychology, there is an evolutionary aspect. Firms that expanded faster by using leverage – or lenders that had looser lending standards – will push out stodgier firms by outperforming. So even if regulators and some banking personnel try pushing back against loosening lending standards, they will be proven wrong by the benign actual outcomes.

Furthermore, the act of debt-driven expansion is self-reinforcing. We can see this from the Kalecki profit equation – which Minsky worked into his theory. Rising investment raises profits. In addition, Minsky worked with a "two price" system: output for current consumption was priced as a markup over costs (which is usual for post-Keynesians), but assets that could be held through time were priced differently. The value of these assets depends on highly uncertain future profits. If things go well, optimism about the future will rise – as will the expected value of the assets. Naturally, the demand for investment goods will rise as well.

Agent-Based Modelling

The most natural way to formalise this theory is via an agent-based model. We simulate the economy by having a large number of "agents" that act independently. We make the willingness to take on leverage vary across agents, and see whether the economy becomes dominated by the agents with the least aversion to risk. The 2011 paper by Chiarella and Di Guilmi[58] provides an example of this approach. In their approach, they have a large number of firms, and the firms jump between two modes of financing (corresponding to speculative and Ponzi financing).

However, agent-based modelling was not computationally feasible when Minsky started his work, and so we are left with a looser aggregated theory. We use this backstory to motivate a drift towards greater risk-taking at the aggregate level. As an example, take the arguments by Minsky in "Financial Instability: a Restatement":[59]

> *The mix of hedge, speculative, and Ponzi finance in existence at any time reflects the history of the economy and the effect of historical developments upon the state of long-term expectations....* <u>*As the*</u> *ratio of speculative and Ponzi units increase in the total financial*

58   Chiarella, Carl, and Corrado Di Guilmi. "The financial instability hypothesis: A stochastic microfoundation framework." *Journal of Economic Dynamics and Control* 35.8 (2011): 1151-1171.

59   On page 106 of *Can It Happen Again?* by Hyman P. Minsky.

structure of an economy, the economy becomes increasingly sensitive to interest rate variations. ...

(One may note Minsky's use of the word "units" in this text. If "agent-based models" had been named "unit-based models," some of his writing would perhaps be more suggestive to modern readers. There is a technical note about his aggregation argument at the end of this section.)

If we want to stick to aggregated models, we either need to have a drift in parameter values motivated by these arguments or we could split some of the aggregates into sub-groups that pursue different levels of leverage. (This would be halfway between a fully aggregated model and an agent-based model.) Since national accounts data are not organised in this fashion, only the aggregated data generated by the model could be compared to real world data. If the belief that the more leveraged firms will expand faster were correct, the aggregate would drift towards higher leverage. However, this understates the effect, as behavioural patterns can shift, and previously low-risk firms decide to join the high-risk group. Such behavioural changes can only be easily dealt with in an agent-based model.

The acceptance of Minsky's theory to a certain extent depends upon one's willingness to accept agent-based models or using qualitative arguments to explain a drift in behavioural parameters. The neoclassical preference was for behavioural parameters that are fixed, hence his theories were not embraced (until the Financial Crisis shook up macroeconomics).[60] Since I have no strong objections to model parameters drifting in this fashion, I do not see a need to chase after agent-based modelling techniques to formalise the theory.

If we accept the Financial Instability Hypothesis, it is not hard to see how a recession develops. The propensity to invest using borrowed money rises over time for both businesses and households. Previous successes validate previous borrowing. However, the reduction in the margins of safety means that some borrowers hit cash problems – either due to some "external shock" disrupting their plans, or a speculative expan-

---

60   This preference is justifiable if one wants to build a model that can be fit to data; if the parameters are moving, we cannot hope to estimate their values using econometric techniques. However, my argument is that since we expect such models will not fit the data in the first place, the inability to use econometric techniques is the least of our worries.

sion was not economically justified. These localised failures create expenditure cutbacks that then ripple through the system. A downward spiral in activity starts, which is only arrested by the various stabilisers in the system (automatic stabilisers that are the result of government policy or the structure of capitalism, or discretionary counter-cyclical policies).

Stability is Destabilising

We can now see one way in which stability is destabilising. An environment with low economic volatility allows higher risk agents to validate their borrowing plans – causing borrowing to drift in a more aggressive direction.

U.S. Mortgage Debt Service Ratio*

*% of disposable income. (Fed BoG via FRED.)

U.S. mortgage debt interest service ratio

Empirically, the story appears to fit the observed data. Unfortunately, an in-depth analysis would require access to detailed statistics on the composition of debt markets. We could look at debt outstanding data (which are available in flow of funds data), but those data are affected by the level of interest rates and income levels. The figure above is one of the few sources in the public domain that are suited for our purposes. It depicts the mortgage servicing cost as a percentage of disposable income for U.S. consumers. The chart starts in 1980 – the point in time where ultra-high interest rates were used to crush inflation. This dampened "animal spirits" in mortgage borrowing, but they later recovered during the 1980s. Mortgage debt service levels rose until the recession of the early 1990s – a recession that was associated with regional housing bear markets, and the Savings and Loan Crisis.

During the 1990s, the debt service ratio was stable, partly courtesy of falling interest rates and financial innovations. During that era, increased competition among mortgage lenders (and technological efficiency improvements) made refinancing of conventional 30-year mortgages in response to lower mortgage rates common. (The author is unaware of other countries that allow refinancing on such advantageous terms for consumers.) However, the gains from falling interest rates were largely spent by the mid-2000s, while mortgage borrowing and lending became increasingly aggressive. As is well known, this came to an end during the Financial Crisis, and mortgage servicing dropped to the early 1980s levels.

As my qualitative story indicates, we cannot rely on mechanical models that assume unchanged behavioural patterns; historical events modify behaviour. As Minsky's historical analysis noted, the Great Depression damped risk-taking behaviour for decades. This data set does not go as far back, but we can infer behavioural pattern changes after the Savings and Loan Crisis and the Financial Crisis.

In order to delve further into disruptions to the cycle, we need to look at the evolution of the financial system, which is discussed in the next section.

In conclusion, if we want to formalise the Financial Instability Hypothesis, the most natural way would be to look at agent-based models. However, if one is willing to be somewhat less formal, we can interpret it through an investment-accelerator model with drifting behavioural parameters, much like Minsky did.

Technical Note

The question arises: is it reasonable to draw a connection between Minsky's arguments and a more formal agent-based model? I would argue that it is. Let us assume that we have disaggregated the business sector into N firms, each with different behavioural parameters, based on where they fit in the hedge-speculative-Ponzi spectrum. Let us assume that the model is set up so that the key behavioural parameter is the propensity to borrow to finance fixed investment. (In many models, this would actually be two decisions: the propensity to invest and how to finance fixed investment. For simplicity, let us collapse that to a single parameter.) If we assume that we are in an expansion, and no firms fail, aggregate behaviour is the sum (or weighted average, depending on the variable) of the individual firm's behaviour. As such, the weighted size of each behavioural type will determine the observed propensity to borrow to invest. We know from microeconomic principles that if the firms are profitable, the more-leveraged firms will have a greater return on equity and will grow faster (since they access more borrowed capital). Therefore, the observed aggregate weightings will shift towards a higher propensity to borrow. (Such a shift matches the quoted discussion by Minsky). It is not until we hit firm failures (presumably in a recession) that the riskier firms will be culled, returning the propensity to borrow to a more conservative level. Although this argument relies on some strong assumptions (e.g., no failures within the expansion), it seems obvious that it is not worthwhile spending too much time trying to formalise the argument.

An alternative way of looking at the previous discussion is that the borrower evolution side of the Financial Instability Hypothesis is an *emergent* property of agent-based models. We just need two properties. Firstly, the model aggregates into something resembling an investment-accelerator model. (I would argue that this is necessary for a "plausible" model, as it is implied by accounting identities, the Kalecki Profit equation, and "stylised facts" about investment behaviour). The next property is that we should expect business failures to be clustered around recessions – a behaviour that matches another stylised fact about bankruptcy statistics.

5.3   Financial Instability Hypothesis – Lenders

The evolution of the financial sector in response to economic incentives and historical experience is the other key leg of Minsky's Financial Instability Hypothesis. It lacks the catchy hedge-speculative-Ponzi unit (agent) scheme, and so is less well known. However, it perhaps poses a greater theoretical challenge, particularly to those who believe that only formal mathematical models are "rigorous." The argument is that the financial sector changes the rules of the financing game over time – which invalidates any formal models based on the old rules.

If we look at Minsky's writings on finance, they cover the details of the evolution of the financial system historically. (One of his earliest papers was on the evolution of the fed funds market in the 1950s.)

If one is familiar with fixed income markets and finance, his argumentation is easy to follow, and one can easily draw parallels to contemporary developments. (This probably explains his popularity among market commentators.) Unfortunately, the mass of details is presumably harder to follow for people less familiar with these markets.

Changing Behaviour

Changing behaviour of the financial system poses severe challenges to macro models. We can view macroeconomic models that simulate all aggregated flows in the economy as being akin to video games. (Admittedly, somewhat boring video games.) The Financial Instability Hypothesis can be interpreted as the financial sector is changing the rules of the game while it is underway.

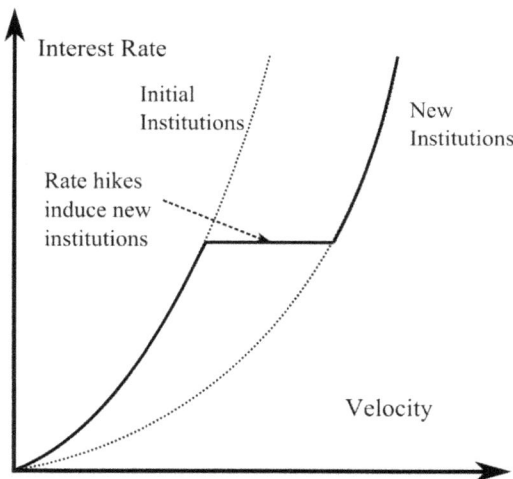

Velocity changing with instituations (from Minsky)

Minsky discussed this in the essay "Central Banking and Money Market Changes" (originally published in 1957), which was reprinted in *Can "It" Happen Again?: Essays on Instability and Finance*. In his example, changing practices in the U.S. banking system allowed banks to reduce the reserves needed to support credit growth, allowing the money velocity/interest rate curve to move. The figure above (based on the figure on page 106 of *Can "It" Happen Again?*) depicts this shift: the curve to the left was the original velocity/interest rate relationship, which jumps to the curve to

the right in response to rising interest rates. This meant that the old estimated relationship between interest rates and velocity has broken down.
If we put aside the usefulness of velocity in analysis (I am skeptical),
we see that estimated model properties will shift because of innovation.

Practices Evolve

If it were just shifting velocity, this may not be too great a worry. However, there is a symbiotic link with the borrower side of the Financial
Instability Hypothesis. Risky borrowers are often unable to access existing financial institutions, due to either regulations or cautious risk
management practices. However, it is usually possible to find someone in the fixed income markets that wants to take on more credit
risk (and quite often has no idea how to evaluate credit risk properly).
This implies that there is a profit to be made to match up the borrower and lender. Innovative credit products spring up to allow this. Since
these necessarily start out small, they initially "fly below the radar."

In other words, the financial system accelerates the tendency for Ponzi
units to expand within aggregates, creating concentrated credit risk, usually out of sight of regulatory bodies. Moreover, there is an evolutionary
effect as well: lenders that extend more risky loans than their peers get better returns, and so they attract more capital. Meanwhile, lenders that have
the greatest tolerance for risk – or the worst capacity to evaluate credit
risk – will end up accumulating large overweight positions in the riski-
est credits. This means that the financial system is accumulating a "tail"
of high-risk firms, probably in areas with little regulation. Since equity is
typically a thin slice of financial firm balance sheets, the system is vulnerable to runs even if a few firms fail. (The ability of derivatives to hide
extreme leverage off balance sheet multiplies these concerns. Aggregated
economic models are unlikely to have a satisfactory explanation for derivatives usage, but agent-based models might be able to incorporate them.)

The tendency for increasing credit risk is tied to the somewhat vague
concept of "liquidity." Within aggregated models, all transactions for a
period happen simultaneously, and the models function without "money"
– actors just need to transact so that all flows net to zero value. This is
not how the real world functions, there must be some form of liquidity
buffer. Some models will create an instrument "money," and insist that actors have a certain level of this instrument to support transactions. How-

ever, this does not match reality, where various credit instruments can be used to undertake transactions. Even if the banking system is used for payments, there is no need that the volume of payments bears any relationship to the size of bank deposits as measured at the end of the day. Increasing reliance on credit instruments for transaction settlement raises the fragility of the financial system – which is inherently hard to model.

Borrower Constraints

Canada: Household Debt To Disposable Income

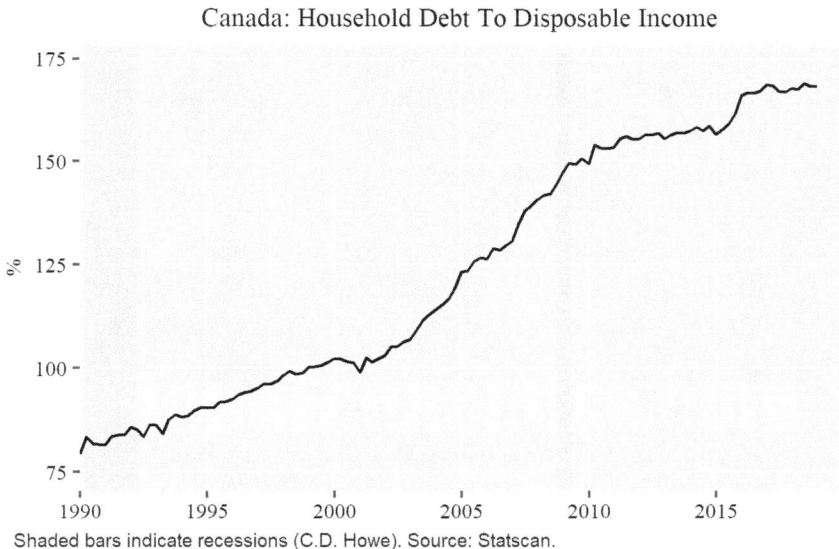

Shaded bars indicate recessions (C.D. Howe). Source: Statscan.

Canadian household debt ratio

The evolution of the financial system would not matter if credit decisions were largely constrained by borrower behaviour. This is the usual tactic of neoclassical models, which assume a "no Ponzi" condition, and households follow some optimising strategy. However, it appears that the lending side is extremely important for the determination of borrowing levels. The figure above depicts the results of the experiment conducted by Canadian policymakers starting in the late 1999s. The regulations controlling borrowing amounts for households were relaxed, and the debt-to-disposable income ratio accelerated upward (after the effects of the technology sector crash faded). Although the downward trend in interest rates helped reduce debt service, this is a classic example of credit growth being induced by relaxed lending standards.

This expansion of debt in Canada was just one part of a global cycle, which ended in the Financial Crisis. For a readable discussion of the details of the financial engineering of the era, I recommend *Econned: How Unenlightened Self Interest Undermined Democracy and Corrupted Capitalism* by Yves Smith (creator of the Naked Capitalism website).[61] For earlier eras, one can consult the chronologies documented by Hyman Minsky. The thing to keep in mind is that Minsky argued that lenders (and borrowers) curb their risk appetite after a major crisis; we need to wait for a new group of employees to take over before the same level of shenanigans is hit again. That said, the financial system is still periodically hit with turbulence as smaller levered financial operations fail.

In summary, financial sector innovation is a critical counterpart to the better-known hedge-speculative-Ponzi borrower scheme. The key is that the financial sector is continuously re-writing the rules of the game, which is a challenge to models that assume behavioural options are fixed.

We will now finish off with several topics that are related to the changes in financial system behaviour but are secondary to the main thrust of the argument.

Why do Financial Innovations Occur?

One question is: why do financial innovations occur at all? The explanation is not at all obvious, if one starts from traditional discussions of the banking system. It is entirely possible for almost all *credit* to be provided by conventional banks (equity either needs to be provided by individuals or via markets), with central government bonds acting as "position making instruments" (Minsky's term for instruments used for liquidity management). Many countries had (or still have) such banking-dominated financial systems.

The reality is that traditional banks have limitations.

- Any entity that does not conform to bankers' views about respectability will not get funding, and so alternate specialty lenders pop up. (The fact that a significant portion of small businesses are financing with credit cards tells us a great deal about the limitations of banks in handling riskier lending.)
- Large borrowers (like multinational corporations) pose concentra-

tion risks to banks, and so they can often only be funded by a consortium of banks. Alternatively, industrial groups are grouped around a funding bank, as was the case in the Japanese *keiretsu* (also known as the "convoy banking system"). The *keiretsu* system was an effective growth strategy, but problems build up over time because of moral hazard.[62]

- The easiest way to make a sale is to lend your customer the money to buy your product – which is effectively what an accounts receivable is. Given the dominance of sales on credit, lenders specialising in funding them is nearly inevitable. (We can lump this under "merchant banking," and we can include entities like firms that factor accounts receivable.)

These lending limitations are not the only factor, and in fact may only be a secondary issue in the current environment. The structure of private sector balance sheets is skewed towards the ownership of large portfolios of financial assets – both pension and insurance funds. Additionally, there is also the desire to hold money market funds. The owners of bond funds typically have actuarial liabilities that are not properly matched against equity holdings, so there is a need for large bond portfolios. Furthermore, these investors have limits for holding concentration, so they cannot hold just bank liabilities. *(That is, we could imagine that banks do all lending to the nonfinancial sector, and investors would hold bank term deposits instead of bonds. However, this would pose unacceptable concentration risks for investors unless those term deposits are guaranteed by the central government.)*

The implication of this balance sheet structure is straightforward – the bond markets have either to fund private sector borrowing either directly or indirectly. The "shadow banking system" evolves in a way to match the actual borrowing needs of the private sector to fit within the constraints of bond financing. For example, asset-backed securities allow small loans to be bundled into a package that can be traded in the wholesale markets.

The other challenge – which ultimately causes a significant portion of distress – is the mismatch between the great desire to hold money market

---

62   For example, see "Moral Hazard under the Japanese 'Convoy' Banking System," by Mark M. Spiegel, Federal Reserve Bank of San Francisco Economic Review (1999). URL: https://www.frbsf.org/economic-research/files/3-13.pdf

maturity instruments versus the small number of borrowers who wish to borrow at such short maturities. The banking system can deal with this mismatch because of being backstopped by the central bank; the non-bank sector naturally lacks such a backstop. Credit lines from banks are used to backstop commercial paper, but those lines are expensive. Eliminating that expense explains one of the drives behind financial innovation – at the cost of vulnerability to runs.

Finally, a good portion of innovations appears to be a way to avoid regulatory costs (such as capital rules) that are typically imposed after a financial crisis.

Is it possible that we can reach a steady state, with regulation perfectly balanced so that all financial activity follows the spirit as well as the letter of the rules? Historically, this has not happened. The profit incentive in the financial sector – plus the political attractiveness of looser lending – overwhelmed regulators. (Any politician that ran on a platform that voters would lose access to easy mortgage credit is likely to have a short career.) We would need some major structural changes in attitudes toward commerce before regulators have the ability to stand against these forces.

Financial Instability Hypothesis Within Models

We will now conclude with a technical discussion of the role of the Financial Instability Hypothesis within economic models. Financial sectors are exceedingly awkward for aggregated economic models, both heterodox as well as neoclassical. Since financial flows are circular, there is no natural barrier to having unlimited cash flows within an economic period within an aggregated (discrete time) model. (An agent-based model might have some limitations if a realistic notion of calendar time is imposed.)

For example, if we look at the simplest stock-flow consistent models, there is nothing stopping wild swings in cash flows from period to period. The next figure shows national output in one such model, generated by allowing the tax rate to jump around each period.[63] The modeller needs to impose some conventions on actor behaviour that force a relatively smooth model solution. (This is not just an issue for stock-flow consistent models, even neoclassical models would exhibit solution instability as the model is re-solved each time period.)

63   The code that generates that plot is found at https://github.com/brianr747/SFC_models/blob/master/sfc_models/examples/scripts/ex20190412_oscillate_wildly.py

National Output With Erratic Taxes

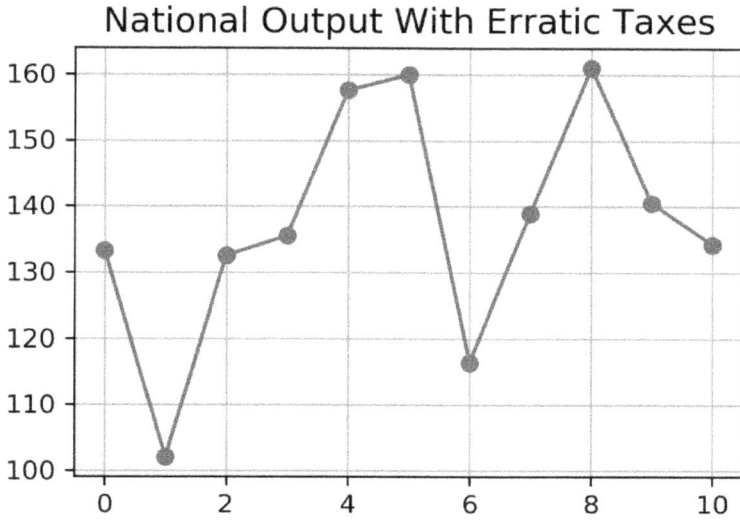

Output with erratic taxes

Government Fiscal Balance Erratic Taxes

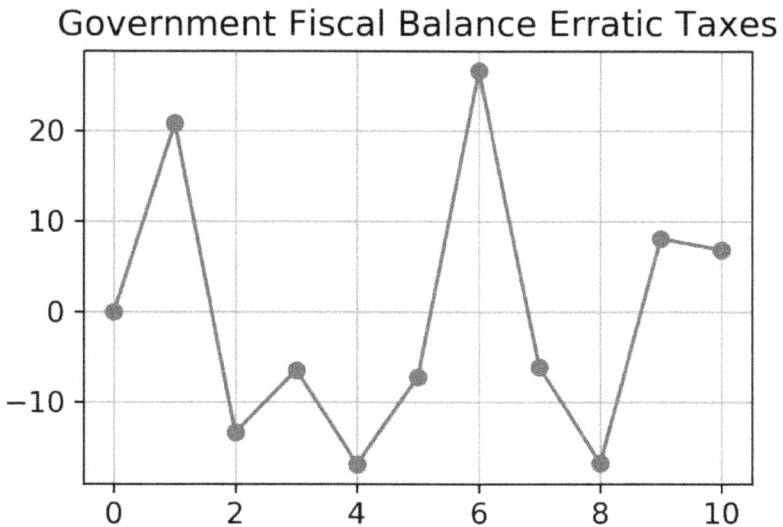

Fiscal balance with erratic taxes

This flexibility is associated with the capacity for lending. Once again, the circular nature of financial flows in the model implies that there are no constraints on the size of lending flows in any period. The above chart depicts the fiscal deficits (as a percentage of GDP) for the previous model with erratic tax rates; the flows in a period do not have to be close to that of the previous period. (There is the concept of loanable funds, which used to be popular in classical economic accounts, which acted as a constraint on lending. Since the idea of loanable funds makes no sense within national accounting concepts, I cannot explain how it was supposed to work.) It should be noted that there could not be a nominal limit on debt growth, since debt growth typically keeps up with nominal GDP growth in high inflation environments. Nevertheless, modellers need to find conventions for behaviour that keep debt growth at plausible levels.

A standard way to constrain the financial sector is to impose capital or reserve constraints on banks in the model. This generates plausible-looking dynamics, and the constraints within the banking sector influence model outcomes. The problem is that we cannot take the model constraints literally, except for financial sectors that are dominated by traditional banking.

- Reserve requirements are problematic, as many countries have abolished reserve requirements. As Minsky discussed, various financial innovations make reserve requirements relatively straightforward to avoid. Furthermore, central banks are forced to create reserves in order for the policy rate to hit their target level, so the banking sector is constrained by interest rate policy, not reserves.[64]
- Capital requirements are more plausible. One issue to note is that regulatory capital is not just equity – there are various subordinated debt instruments that can be included. More importantly, the non-bank financial system does not face capital requirements for the expansion of its balance sheet.

The move to bypass bank capital requirements via securitisations is an important lesson. Attempts to constrain certain forms of lending make them uneconomic, so the private sector moves to alternate arrangements. A model that models the financial sector as a single aggregate with a fixed capital requirement will only work until the point that alternate financial arrangements take over (e.g., securitisations).

As such, we need to disaggregate the financial sector, and allow multi-

---

64   I discuss bank reserves in Chapter 13 of *Abolish Money (From Economics)!*

ple financing instruments. This can be done in stock-flow consistent models, albeit with cumbersome algebra. However, we run into an immediate problem: actors in the model should be immediately aware of all financing options, and exploit each to their maximum potential immediately. Financing practices would not naturally evolve; the financial system has reached full maturity immediately. If one wanted to emulate the growth trajectory of new financing structures, the regulatory burden would need to limit their market share at the beginning, of the simulation, and then relax the burdens. This is actually the opposite of the real-world experience, where novel financing schemes are progressively clamped down on by regulators.

If one wanted to simulate this evolution in a mathematical model, a complex financial sector would be required, probably using an agent-based model. (This complexity would make the model impossible to fit to data, but it might be useful as a theoretical construct, or even in a video game.) All possible financing schemes would be defined by some parameters, and the model would start with a small number of them. As time passes, new potential modes of finance are developed. Since adopting new financing practices requires costly research, take-up of the new modes will be limited. The success of units using the new modes of financing will spawn copycat behaviour, and so its market share grows.

Creating such a model using aggregates would be extremely difficult, but it would not pose too much added complexity for an agent-based model. The plasticity of behaviour would make drawing any conclusions from the model awkward, although it may be useful for seeing how far predictions based on measured aggregates can depart from reality in an environment of financial innovation.

Concluding Remarks

In conclusion, evolution of financial system behaviour amplifies the instability created by changing borrower behaviour. Since the financial sector needs to accommodate aggressive risk-taking by borrowers, the financial evolution cannot be ignored, even though it poses even greater modelling risks.

Finally, one should not approach the Financial Instability Hypothesis as justifying being permanently bearish; the Financial Crisis of 2008 is not going to repeat every few years. People and institutions learn from traumatising events – such as the Great Depression and the Financial Crisis.

From the 1966-2008 period, a certain amount of paranoia was justified: the financial sector did suffer periodic disruptions. However, they were generally not enough to cause global crises that forced a wider re-think of behaviour.

Although memories in finance are short-lived, behaviour is still relatively cautious. (Pockets of zaniness exist, but these are generally not associated with the wholesale funding markets,[65] which are what matters for the economy.) One could argue that the biggest risks that hang over the system are the only sectors/actors that did not have a forced reset after the Financial Crisis (and the follow-up euro sovereign crisis). The author cannot pretend to know whether those sectors are due for a reckoning. Although some look worrisome, it is hard to find policymakers who are complacent about such risks this close to the Financial Crisis.

5.4   Aggregated Continuous Time Models

An alternative approach to economic modelling is to use a continuous time formalism. That is, instead of having a model jump from a discrete time point to another such time point (e.g., months), the time axis is a real variable (and may contain fractional parts). This is the usual standard in physical and engineering models.[66] In the heterodox tradition, Steve Keen is the best-known developer of these models in recent years. He collaborated with Russell Standish to develop the *Minsky* continuous time modelling software package. Other researchers have expanded this work, with the focus on the instability of economies.

Why Continuous Time?

Trond Adresen compares discrete time versus continuous time models in Chapters 2 and 3 of his doctoral thesis – *On the Dynamics of Money Circulation and Debt – A Control Systems Approach* (submitted in October 2018 to the Norwegian University of Science and Technology).

In Section 2.3, Adresen makes a few arguments in favour of continuous time.

65   At the time of editing this text, there was a small disruption in the governmental repo markets. This appears to be purely a technical issue that would at best concern a few money market funds/treasury desks.
66   With the rise of digital electronics, a great deal of engineering is now implicitly discrete time. For example, observations are discretely sampled of continuous physical variables.

- The distinction between stock and flow variables is clear; the variables in the model are stocks, while their rates-of-change are flows. Units for a stock are dollars ($), and flows are ($/time, usually $/year). In a discrete time model, cash flows are aggregated to give a single number which has the same units as a stock ($).
- He cites Steve Keen for noting that continuous time models can easily handle different time scales for reactions.
- He argues that system parameters are invariant for continuous time, while they would vary depending on the length of time step chosen. *(However, I would observe that resampling discrete time systems to different frequencies is commonly done in systems engineering.)*
- He argues that the Dirac delta "function" may be used to model cash flow jumps. *(Although this is true, I would note that a proper mathematical treatment of delta functions is complex. As the scare quotes emphasise, the delta "function" can only be properly understood using measure theory.)*

I would argue that the main advantage of continuous time is that mathematical theory for continuous time dynamic systems is much richer. Since the model state variables follow continuous paths (in the absence of delta functions), we can make mathematical statements about the regions of the state space. For example, we can determine the existence of a limit cycle – a trajectory that variables in a region will converge towards.

My preference is for discrete time models. Appendix A.1 in *An Introduction to SFC Models Using Python* gives a longer version of my arguments, but I will give a short summary. Firstly, I was able to implement models as examples within the *sfc_models* framework. Secondly, most of the literature works with discrete time models. Finally, the mathematical complexity is greatly reduced. For example, if we allowed for random disturbances in the system, the notational complexity explodes. All the variables that depend on the random variables would be non-differentiable almost everywhere – making it hard to define concepts like flows.

Modelling the Financial Instability Hypothesis

One of the earlier papers using this technique was "Financial and Economic Breakdown: Modelling Minsky's 'Financial Instability Hypothesis,'" by Steve Keen.[67] The model is based on the earlier Goodwin model of the trade cycle but adds financial considerations.

If we remove finance from consideration, we end up with the Goodwin model, which can be simulated with two differential equations. The variables that determine behaviour are the wage share of income, and the percentage of the population that is employed. For the parameters used, the resulting model is qualitatively stable; the solution can end up either in an equilibrium point (steady state) or at a *limit cycle*. As the name suggests, a limit cycle is a repeating trajectory to which "nearby" trajectories will tend over time. For example, we could have the business cycle that repeats every five years. Since the economy might be contracting (a recession), this might not meet expectations for what counts as "stable," but it might be considered from a technical sense (since variables are not growing in an unbounded fashion.

The addition of finance changes the picture: the trajectory of economic variables can veer off rapidly in a new direction, even though it had previously been oscillating mildly. The model embeds compounding dynamics that can result in a sector rapidly losing money.

As Keen argues, this provides an alternative way to arrive at Minsky's financial instability hypothesis, without moving towards an agent-based model.

Chaos and Equilibrium

Two topics that come up frequently in the context of the continuous time heterodox research programme are chaos and equilibrium. In addition to Steve Keen referring to these ideas, I have seen the same ideas crop up repeatedly in the writings of others. For a long-time observer, the popularity of these ideas is not too surprising. *Chaos* burst into popular mathematics and in some segments of academia in the 1980s. (Chaos theory was loosely based on some ideas from nonlinear dynamics, and I was in the hard theory wing of nonlinear control theory, so it was in my area of academic expertise.) Meanwhile, heterodox economists have been complaining about the notion of equilibrium in economics for decades.

The interesting argument coming from chaos theory is that one could use it to argue that economic forecasting is nearly impossible. This resem-

67   Finance and Economic Breakdown: Modeling Minsky's "Financial Instability Hypothesis," by Steve Keen. *Journal of Post Keynesian Economics*, Vol. 17, No. 4 (Summer, 1995), pp. 607-635. URL: http://www.jstor.org/stable/4538470

bles my arguments about the difficulty in forecasting recessions. However, I think the case based on chaos theory is weaker than what I am suggesting.

I want to emphasise that I am making general remarks aimed at the popular use of chaos theory and equilibrium critiques, and not aimed at any one author's discussions. In most cases I have seen, various assertions are made about chaos theory in passing, and then the discussion leaps to another topic. In my view, it is much harder to draw strong conclusions from chaos theory than the popular accounts suggest.

I would summarise the usual argument based on chaos theory as follows. If we look at linear systems, they can be easily divided into two classes of models: stable and unstable. The key property of unstable systems is that their state trajectories "blow up" (head off to infinity) with a near certain probability. (This assumes any form of randomness hits the system. If there are no sources of randomness, it may be possible for a system to sit in an unstable equilibrium forever. For example, an object could be balanced on a knife point, and could sit there until some random breeze causes it to shift out of balance.)

Once we introduce nonlinear dynamics, we can get almost any behaviour.[68] In particular, we can get a nice, well-behaved cyclic behaviour – which gives the impression of dynamic stability if we think in terms of a linear model – that then proceeds to blow up in an unstable fashion. The part of "chaos" that captured the imagination of many was the realisation that tiny deviations in the initial conditions can lead to very large deviations in later behaviour. (There was an extremely popular anecdote about a butterfly flapping its wings in some country that leads to small deviations in air pressure that later "cause" a hurricane somewhere else. Based on my limited and rusty knowledge of thermodynamics and energy conservation laws, I would argue that "causality" seems to be a misnomer in that story.)

If we accept that economies in some sense exhibit "chaotic" properties, this spells doom for attempts to treat economic forecasting as a naïve "scientific" exercise. The period of stable behaviour will likely cause us to misdiagnose systems parameters, and the sensitivity to initial conditions

68   The critique that I and others made about chaos theory in the 1980s and early 1990s was that the observation that nonlinear systems could do practically anything was obvious to anyone who carefully read the foundational works in nonlinear dynamical systems.

means that forecasts will fail.

Unfortunately, I see two issues with the previous line of argument.

1. The most important problem is that even if we write down a model for the economy that has some features that match those of the real world, it still does not mean that the model is valid. There could be a similar model without "chaotic properties" that does just as good a job of fitting reality.

2. Secondly, the sensitivity to initial conditions is not a major concern if we continuously update the estimate of the state of the system. Yes, estimation errors will grow, but the magnitude of the errors will be capped by the arrival of new information. All that we can say is that long-range forecasting is impossible, but that is obviously true for any system that is being hit by "random" external shocks. We will still have acceptable near-run forecasts (with errors of a magnitude related to the magnitude of the external shocks).

If we turn to the various debates about economic theory, these notions lead to some criticism of neoclassical theory. For example, in Chapter 2 of the book *Debunking Economics,*[69] Steve Keen attacks mainstream undergraduate economics for focussing on linear differential equations. As noted earlier, linear systems analysis gives a misleading picture of the stability properties of systems. I am unsure that this critique hits the mark, however.

If we look at the so-called "log-linear" dynamic stochastic general equilibrium (DSGE) models that were popular in the era before the Financial Crisis, the criticisms about relying on linear models are entirely correct. However, it should be noted that the literature was moving towards nonlinear models, and so the criticism could be viewed as dated.

Much more problematic is the notion of "equilibrium." Unfortunately, economists have appropriated a term from dynamic systems theory (and/or the physical science) and are using it in a fashion that does not match usage there.

- In dynamic systems theory, an equilibrium is a point in the state space at which the state remains over time. For example, if the

69   *Debunking Economics – Revised, Expanded and Integrated Edition: The Naked Emperor Dethroned?,* by Steve Keen, Zed Books Ltd, 2011. ISBN: 8791780322209.

state of the system refers to an object's position and velocity, an equilibrium is a point at which the object remains motionless over time.

- In neoclassical theory, it is difficult to find a clean definition of an equilibrium. However, from context, it is what other fields of applied mathematics would refer to as a system solution: a set of present and expected future prices at which supply equals demand. (By way of background, expected future prices are like financial futures prices: they may refer to prices in the future, but their prices are determined in the present.) Historically, they thought of prices jumping up and down in order to reach that solution – which is a process in time – but any such price movements do not appear in the model mathematics.

It is safe to say that most of the articles published on neoclassical modelling skip over the technical details of the determination of the model solution. If we wish to invoke a concept from economics, there is a revealed preference here – the subject of model solutions ("equilibrium") is not worth delving into in depth. Instead, the focus is on what principles can be inferred from the model. As a result, it could be argued the complaints from people like Steve Keen (and myself) are somehow missing the point. Given the extreme gap between those viewpoints, I will defer discussion of this topic until Volume II.

Are Continuous Time Models Too Smooth?

One of my concerns with continuous time models is that they are effectively models of an instantaneous present: all model actors are reacting instantly to current state variables. The way they react is continuous, and so we end up with smooth state trajectories.

A discrete time model offers a lumpier decision process. Actors have information on the current period (and the past), and are extrapolating one time period (month/quarter) into the future (at least). If the previous period's decision turns out to have been ill-advised, they may need to make a strong corrective action in the current period. This creates a potential for greater jumps in behaviour – which matches the sharp jumps seen around recessions.

Although it is unrealistic to have all actors make decisions at the same time point, there are limits to reaction time. Although some digital platforms can hire "contractors" in real time (as can some industries with casual workforces), most employers cannot calibrate their hiring decisions at a high frequency. As such, continuous time models allow too much decision-making flexibility. If such flexibility were the norm, it is unclear why firms would make erroneous decisions that lead to recessions, instead they would react quickly and take less drastic measures.

Concluding Remarks

Whether one uses continuous time models is a stylistic decision. The emphasis on dynamic instability in recent work is certainly interesting. However, discrete time offers a more tractable environment to model forward-looking behaviour. Although I am not a fan of neoclassical models, one cannot dispute the importance of forward-looking behaviour for things like decisions for fixed investment. Even if the modelling of forward planning is too simplistic in off-the-shelf stock-flow consistent models, we have the capacity to insert more complex decision rules and examine the effect on model behaviour.

5.5   External Financial Constraints and Crises

If we look at the full history of financial crises around the world, one could argue that crises related to external debt and/or fixed exchange rates are dominant. Such crises could represent an entire chapter of this book. However, I will only offer a brief overview of the subject. From the perspective of recession forecasting, the addition of a fixed exchange rate regime adds a new wrinkle to analysis: when might the peg fail, causing a crisis? As I will discuss below, this is quite different than an analysis of the domestic economy, which one might hope is amenable to something resembling econometric analysis.

It should be noted that this is a topic that is a source of deep controversy between Modern Monetary Theory and other groups of post-Keynesians. However, my experience is with floating currency developed sovereigns, and as I discuss here, there are not much in the way of historical precedents of truly external crises for such countries.

Fixed Exchange Rates: They Eventually Fail

A fixed exchange rate system is where a country declares that its local currency can be converted into another instrument, typically either gold or a

foreign currency. If we look at the history from after the end of World War
I, being able to convert to gold was largely the same thing as pegging to
one of the major currencies (since they were all nominally pegged to gold).

It is very easy for such systems to break down. If a country has a current account deficit, it implies that there must be a corresponding capital
inflow (in a broad sense) as a result of accounting identities. More simply,
if a local entity buys something from a foreigner, they need to buy the foreign currency to import it – which implies the need for an offsetting purchase of the local currency. That is, one of the following typically occurs.

- Foreign entities are buying financial instruments in the local
  economy; quite often fixed income instruments. This is essentially the same thing as "buying the local currency," since that
  is typically executed by buying financial instruments (or making
  deposits in local banks); buying and selling of notes and coins
  (e.g., dollar bills) is relatively small when compared to cross-
  border flow.
- Local entities are borrowing overseas (which can be viewed as
  functionally equivalent to the previous point).
- Local entities sell foreign assets and use the proceeds to "buy
  the local currency."
- If the following are not enough to balance the foreign exchange
  market, the central bank needs to intervene in the market: buying or selling reserve currencies or gold in order to buy back its
  local currency.

The final possibility – central bank intervention – is what differenti-
ates a peg from a floating currency. During normal conditions, market
participants expect the peg to hold. When the currency gets near the limit
of its trading band (in practice, currencies are allowed to trade in a range
around the peg value), private sector actors will step in to buy/sell in such
a way as to move the currency back towards the centre. For example, if
the price is near the low end, traders will buy. If the peg was credible, this
was a low risk trade: the central bank would prevent any further fall, while
it could rise towards the middle of the peg band again. As such, the peg
could remain in place, even though the central bank does not intervene.

The problem is the credibility of the peg. If a currency is strengthening, there are no problems: the central bank buys foreign currencies (or

gold) with domestic currency to keep its value from appreciating. Since the domestic currency is just a liability of the central bank, there is no limit to this process. The problem is currency weakness. The central bank needs to have something to sell in order to intervene with either gold or a foreign currency (currency reserves). When they run out, they can no longer intervene. This means that the currency will have to fall to a level where supply and demand in the private sector is matched. (In practice, pegs are typically broken before those reserves run out.)

The previous discussion was quite loose, but neoclassical economists have formalised this discussion with mathematical models, such as the analysis of self-fulfilling currency runs.[70] The process seems similar to other market processes (such as self-fulfilling runs on borrowers), so it seems to be a distraction to chase after the details of the formalisation here.

Since central banks can stop appreciation, if all countries trusted each other completely, they could always intervene to allow the peg values to hold. In practice, such unlimited trust does not exist, and so foreign central banks will allow foreign currencies to suffer runs and have the peg break on the other side.

The problems posed by a peg breaking are quite clear. In addition to the policy reaction (discussed next), domestic entities may be borrowing in a "hard" foreign currency. If the value of the currency collapses versus those hard currencies, the value of the loan rises markedly in the local currency. This will cause financial distress, and thus a financial crisis.

Recessions Ahead of Peg Breaking

However, peg breaking is the end game. Countries typically preserved parities by fiscal austerity policies – cutting spending, raising taxes, thus reducing domestic demand, and in turn, imports. This should improve the trade balance, which allows the country to rebuild foreign currency reserves. The other avenue is to raise interest rates, which will attract foreign capital inflows, and presumably slow the economy (as will be discussed in Volume II). Although it is unclear why raising interest rates will raise a currency value in a floating rate regime, there is a mechanism for it to support a currency with a peg. So long as the peg holds, local bonds

70   One early paper is "Rational and Self-Fulfilling Balance-of-Payments Crises" by Maurice Obstfeld, NBER Working Paper 1486, November 1984. URL: https://www.nber.org/papers/w1486.pdf

with a higher yield will outperform lower-yielding foreign bonds. (For a floating currency, currency movements normally swamp the effect of yield differentials on short holding periods.) This creates capital inflows – which balance the currency market without central bank intervention.

Fiscal austerity and raising interest rates are conventionally viewed as a policy tightening, and hence can cause a recession. These are policy-induced recessions, and so seem to be somewhat forecastable. Therefore, this perhaps is a strong counterexample to my arguments that recessions are hard to forecast. If we can forecast the need for a policy tightening to preserve a currency peg based on trends in the currency reserve position, we could presumably forecast the recession.

Even if we accept that argument, we are faced with the hard-to-forecast issue of political risk. Rather than absorb a recession – or a depression – policymakers can abandon the currency peg. Judging the likelihood of such an outcome is perhaps a job for analysts of political economy, and not amenable to econometrics.

The previous summary captures the main issues around fixed exchange rates in this context; beyond that, we need to dig into institutional detail. Those details are important for analysing the risk of crisis or recession. In the modern era, the euro area and developing countries give us examples. If we look further back, the relationship between the interwar Gold Standard and the Great Depression gives us a large data set on the interactions. My thinking is largely based on the analysis found in the text *Golden Fetters* by Barry Eichengreen.[71] It should be noted that there are many defenders of the Gold Standard, who argue that the interwar problems were due to other policy errors, and/or problems with fractional reserve lending.

Crises in Floating Currencies?

There is not much doubt that fixed exchange rates are associated with marked recession risks that are associated with the regime. The controversy lies more in the area of floating currencies. Can the external sector induce a crisis that leads to recession? For example, if one follows the business press, one argument that pops up periodically is that foreign borrowers own a disproportionate share of U.S. securities, and

71   *Golden Fetters: The Gold Standard and the Great Depression 1919-1939,* by Barry Eichengreen, Oxford University Press, 1992. ISBN: 0-19-510113-8.

that there will be a "buyer's strike," and an associated financial crisis.

From a more academic perspective, there were considerable worries about financial imbalances and the "unsustainable" nature of the American current account deficit. It has been argued that the problem was not that economists did not predict the 2008 Financial Crisis, rather they predicted the wrong crisis.[72] Since I do not see much value in taking apart forecasts made a decade earlier, I will not dwell on that point.

In my view, searching for an external sector culprit behind a financial crisis is not needed – since the factors leading to the crisis do not materially depend upon the nationality of the sources of finance. My reasoning is straightforward. Firstly, floating currencies do not fall forever; at some valuation they become attractive and the market reaches a new flow equilibrium Secondly, currency volatility prevents the buildup of positions by investors who are concerned about currency risk in the first place. I discuss these in turn.

Currencies Eventually Stabilise

An exchange rate is a relative price: one currency unit for another. If we look at the post-1990 period, inflation rates in the developed countries have been quiescent, bouncing around 2% for most countries. As such, each currency has relatively stable purchasing power for domestic goods and services, including the cost of wages.

The stability of wages has one side effect: if a currency falls rapidly versus its developed peers, the cost of wages falls relative to other countries. This drops input costs for production relative to other countries. And even if imported inputs rise in price in domestic terms due to the drop in the exchange rate, those input costs are unaffected when expressed in terms of the foreign currency unit.

The result is that domestic exporters suddenly have greater prospective profit margins versus their international peers. This will have two effects: buoy the attractiveness of the local equity market and attract investment inflows (either reallocations of capital by multinationals or foreign direct investment).

These capital flows (and the prospect of future flows) help put a floor

72   For example, see "Macroeconomics Predicted the Wrong Crisis," by Adam Tooze, September 10, 2018. URL: https://www.ineteconomics. org/perspectives/blog/macroeconomics-predicted-the-wrong-crisis

under the domestic currency. This helps explain why there have been no cases of developed countries' currencies going to zero in the foreign exchange marketplace.

Who Takes Foreign Exchange Risk?

One empirical regularity that is often overlooked: the general absence of defaults caused by exchange rate movements in developed countries. The explanation is a reversal of one of Minsky's catch phrases: instability is stabilising.

Borrowers are aware of the risks of borrowing in a foreign currency. To the extent that it is done, it is done on a currency-hedged basis. These hedges may be outright hedges, or the implicit hedges created by having foreign operations. For example, Canadian firms operating in the United States, or with significant U.S. dollar denominated revenue, may borrow in U.S. dollars, thus reducing their foreign exchange risk. Obviously, some firms can default, but defaults happen for any number of reasons. (The situation in Iceland in 2008 was a fiasco, but it is impossible to characterise the Icelandic firms as being run by responsible grownups.)

Owners of financial assets have a mixed picture.

- Banks balance sheets are almost entirely hedged. They may run foreign exchange risks that appear large to individuals, but those risks are very small versus the size of their balance sheets. If we look at the Financial Crisis, the problem faced by banks was that many foreign banks were holding U.S. dollar-denominated assets, but their deposit base was in foreign currencies. The willingness of counterparties to offer them U.S. dollar wholesale funding or via hedges (cross-currency basis swaps) waned, and they were forced to turn to their central banks' swap lines with the U.S. Federal Reserve. That is, the current account deficit country had to extend backdoor bailouts to banks in other countries – including the trade juggernaut, Germany.

- Bond funds are slaves to their investment mandates. At present, the bulk of bond funds are being held for liability management purposes, particularly by pension funds and insurance funds. These funds are required to manage their portfolios against their projected future cash flows – which are in the domestic currency. Multi-currency funds exist but are a hard sell in a world of low yields. The funds with domestic benchmarks may hold foreign currency bonds, but they do so in a hedged fashion. This need for hedging is the counterpart to the desire of issuers to hedge their borrowings. Offsetting flows allows borrowers and lenders to diversify their sources/sinks for funding – although these do not provide net currency flows. The international bond market is mainly for allocating credit and duration risk; the effect on currency flows is smaller.

- Individuals may hold foreign currency bonds; Japan is well known for having retail investors that gamble on foreign currency debt. Although these exposures are unhedged, they are quite small relative to institutional flows.
- Foreign exchange funds, and currency overlays on portfolios do take currency positions, but their balance sheet capacity is still relatively small when compared to gross capital flows.
- Foreign official currency reserve managers bear currency risk on their portfolios. However, as governmental institutions, they are normally spared the worries about mark-to-market. Instead, their objective is to manage their exchange rate, typically trying to keep it at a level that facilitates exports. The other constraint on their actions is that the largest reserve managers are trapped in the markets with the deepest bond markets (notably the United States). Even if they really liked New Zealand bonds, they cannot do too much about that view.
- The residual class of investors are the ones who absorb most of the currency risk: equity funds. International equity funds are popular, and they are rarely currency hedged. Courtesy of buoyant equity valuations, the equity market has the heft to absorb cross-currency flows from trade.

The reality that a falling currency helps local equity valuations is the secret sauce behind the resilience of floating currencies. To use an expression from Canadian/American football, floating currencies bend, but do not break.[73]

---

73   A football defence that "bends, but does not break" is one that is willing to give up short gains, but prevent big plays. It forces the opposing offence to slowly grind down the field, waiting for a miscue that forces a punt.

No Firm Dividing Line Between Domestic and External Crises

The nature of modern financial market behaviour makes it hard to draw a line between an "external" and "domestic" private sector financial crisis: foreign and domestic investors are commingled across the globe already. If a sector of the economy launches an ill-fated investment scheme that draws in credulous investors, the odds are that those investors are from all over the globe. Since those investors have currency hedges in place, their concern is not the value of the currency, rather it is the prospect of credit losses. The tendency to panic at the prospect of credit losses is one of those wonderful properties that are shared by all human beings, regardless of their nationality.

For this reason, searching for an "external" cause of a financial crisis is largely a waste of time: the crisis will happen because some class of borrowers incurred debts that cannot be repaid. The reasons why they cannot be repaid will depend upon domestic conditions; the source of their lending is only a detail of interest to purveyors of financial horror stories.

Events in the Financial Crisis do point to a counterexample to this logic: domestic financial institutions can grow out of control in foreign markets, such as the Icelandic banks. They fail because of events outside the domestic economy. However, such an event is largely driven by regulatory failure, and not conditions in the domestic economy. The only way to diagnose such problems is to understand the risks of the financial institutions – but those risks are almost certainly being obscured by said institutions.

Policymaker Panic

We now turn to the possibility of a governmental financial (fiscal) crisis. From a practical perspective, the main risk associated with a floating currency is the probability of policymakers panicking because of a falling currency value. For example, Canadian policymakers were worried about the falling Canadian dollar in the early 1990s. (One could point to the United Kingdom going to the IMF in the 1970s, but that was clouded by fixed exchange rate concerns.)

The usual panic responses are "emergency rate hikes" and/or cutting spending. Any resulting recession is policy-induced. Although the business press might write about an external "fiscal crisis," the reality is that foreigners have no more power to force an involuntary bankruptcy than domestic government bond buyers.

Nevertheless, we need to be realistic about the politics. There is a large contingent of politicians/economists that want to see government spending cut, and they will seize any excuse to justify those cuts. We need look no further than the voluntary fiscal austerity policies pursued in the United Kingdom after the Financial Crisis as an example of such political opportunism.

Therefore, predicting such a self-imposed recession is a question of political economy. Certain governments might panic in response to a weaker currency, causing a deep recession. Other governments will just sail through the currency weakness, waiting for valuations to revert. As such, predicting such recessions is not going to be easy based on econometric analysis.

Finally, one can imagine a country being cut off from foreign trade as a result of some geopolitical crisis and forced to defend the currency in order to be able to pay for strategic imports. Although possible, this is yet another question of politics, and not econometric analysis.

Ultimately, Political Risk

In summary, the risks around financial crises (including fiscal crises) that are due to the external sector end up being political: will the authorities induce a recession to defend a peg, or let it break? Will a floating currency sovereign government panic and raise rates/cut spending in order to defend its currency value? Economic analysis can extrapolate trends and tell us what the economic pressures are on the government, but how policymakers react is not amenable to solution in a mathematical model.

5.6   Popular Austrian Business Cycle Theory

The Austrian school of economics is an unabashedly free market-oriented school of thought that can be lumped in with "heterodox" economics. This free market bias probably explains its popularity within financial market commentary – a popularity that is far greater than its influence in academia at present. Since this popular version of Austrian economics is what is most often encountered, this is what I will discuss. If we focus solely on recession forecasting, I see considerable overlap in the mechanisms discussed, as we can easily re-interpret Austrian arguments into a post-Keynesian framework without doing too much violence to thinking. (This overlap is not true for other aspects of the theory.)

I have little doubt that my summary here would not be enough to satisfy an Austrian economist. However, if I attempted to delve into the subject deeper, we run into several problems. The first is that the popular Austrian writing is quite often divorced from a coherent body of theory. Assertions are made and backed up by picking quotations from earlier academic Austrians in a haphazard fashion. This then runs into the issue that the different academic Austrians disagreed with each other, and so one is stuck with a long-winded examination of each diverging view. Finally, I am not very sympathetic to the Austrian theoretical positions and would then feel a need to present criticisms of these views. By just looking at the practical similarities between the Austrian and post-Keynesian views on the causes of recession, I can largely sidestep my concerns. However, it should be emphasised that I am not arguing that Austrian economics is "just" post-Keynesian theory with a free market make-over.

Groupings

For simplicity, I will divide Austrian economists into three groups.

1. The first group are the classical Austrian economists (Hayek, von Mises, etc.). Many were of Austrian origin, hence the name for the school of thought. It is unclear to the author how internally consistent the various authors' theories are; like the literary post-Keynesians, there are some serious theoretical divides between the non-mathematical discussions. The key point is that they are long dead, and much of the literature is from the pre-Keynesian era.

2. The second group are modern academics. These academics have embraced the use of some mathematical models.

3. The last group is the topic of conversation: those who follow a popularised version of Austrian economics. This group is numerous in financial market commentary, and has a large presence on the internet. This group usually appeals to quotations to the classical Austrian theory. (I cannot recall seeing references to more recent academic work, other than studies of economic history.)

When I worked in finance, I read a great deal of Austrian market commentary. Like almost all financial market commentary – including most of my own commentary – the theory is not formalised. For example, I wrote a brief review of the book *Paper Money Collapse: The Folly of Elastic Money* by Detlev Schlichter. This is a book on forecast economic/financial events written by a financial market professional from an Austrian perspective without any formal models.[74]

Recession Narrative

I will now attempt to summarise what appears to be the underlying themes that appear in popular Austrian accounts. (I compare my summary to a book by Rothbard, as discussed below.) The reader will need to keep in mind that I have no sympathies for the Austrian political platform. Furthermore, I am not attempting to use preferred Austrian phrasing; I am translating what I have read into my usual writing style.

The first theoretical tic of popular Austrian theory is that the usual starting point is a hypothetical world where money is 100% gold-backed, that is, fractional reserve banking is prohibited. Although starting with pure commodity money could be justified as a theoretical simplification, this is also a strong policy bias of Austrians. The result is that if one scans the popular Austrian literature, forecasts of banking system collapses and/ or the demise in hyperinflation is not hard to find (as the title of the book *Paper Money Collapse* suggests). Given that a country like Canada has had a floating currency since 1950 (with an 8-year interruption in the 1960s),[75] even if fiat currencies are inevitability doomed, they can outlast most short positions. The challenge for an analyst of Austrian sympathies is to avoid the dreaded "stopped clock" syndrome.[76]

The emphasis on sound money results in a good deal of discussion of inflation. The *Cantillon Effect* is discussed extensively. The concept is straightforward – the first people to borrow money drive up the price of goods, disadvantaging those who are slower to take advantage of the expansion of the money supply. Unfortunately, it is not obvious to the

74   The review "What Can We Learn From Austrian Economics?" is available at http://www.bondeconomics.com/2014/12/what-can-we-learn-from-austrian.html

75   As noted in the speech "Taking Precautions: The Canadian Approach to Foreign Reserves Management," by deputy governor Timothy Lane (given on February 6, 2019) https://www.bankofcanada.ca/2019/02/taking-precautions-canadian-approach-foreign-reserves-management.

76   "A stopped clock is right twice a day."

author how to test this theory. In any event, that topic is not of immediate relevance to the discussion of recessions.

From a practical perspective, the 100% gold-backed currency starting point has a severe defect – we live in societies dominated by flexible credit and fractional reserve banking. If we go back in time, we see that even the Romans had credit money (the economic equivalent of fractional reserve lending)[77], despite popular accounts that Roman commerce was conducted with metal coins. The imperative of capitalism is to sell goods and services at a profit, and the path of least resistance for a sale is to lend the customer the money to purchase the product. As a result, economic forces push towards flexible credit relationships. However, a debate about a world without fractional reserve banking is a distraction from what is important for our present discussion: the concept of the "free market interest rate." This is the rate of interest that would result if money were 100% backed by gold. This concept is critical for the business cycle theory and will be discussed later.

If we want to discuss the real world, we arrive at the popular Austrian concept of *malinvestment*. This is a simplified version of more a formal Austrian Business Cycle Theory. However, my understanding of the formal theory is that there are multiple versions, so I will stick with a popular version that is closer to what one would encounter in financial market commentary.

If we turn to section B ("Credit Expansion and the Business Cycle") in Chapter 11 of Murray N. Rothbard's *Man, Economy, and State with Power and Market*[78], we get a textual description of the business cycle. The key to the analysis is that capital goods are viewed as a way of saving time in the

77   The assertion made is my characterisation of the discussion within the essay "The Nature of Roman Money," by W.V. Harris, found in the book **The Monetary Systems of the Greeks and Romans** (edited by W.V. Harris). Oxford University Press, 2008. ISBN: 978-0-19-958671-4. The essay starts with the observation that the two million **sesterces** payment made in the Kubrick movie **Spartacus** – which was depicted as two smallish sacks – would have required two sacks of 965 kilograms of coins.

78   **Man, Economy, and State with Power and Market (Second Edition)**, Murray N. Rothbard, Scholar's Edition, Ludwig von Mises Institute, 2009. ISBN: 978-1-933550-27-5.

production of consumer goods; the capital goods are organised in layers of complexity. He writes:

> *We have already seen in chapter 8 what happens when there is net sav-ing-investment: an increase in the ratio of gross investment to consumption in the economy. Consumption expenditures fall, and the price of consum-ers' goods fall. On the other hand, the production structured is lengthened, and the prices of the original factors specialized in the higher stages rises.*

He makes arguments about equilibrium, and then:

> *Thus, an increase in saving resulting from a fall in time pref-erences leads to a fall in the interest rate and another sta-ble equilibrium with a longer and narrower production structure.*

One could perhaps attempt to validate his statements about price and interest rate shifts versus data, but I will put that aside. What we are inter-ested in is the following argument.

> *The market therefore reacts to the distortion of the free-market in-terest rate by proceeding to revert to that very rate. The distortion caused by credit expansion deceives businessmen into believing that more sav-ings are available and causes them to* malinvest — *to invest in projects that will turn out to be unprofitable when consumers have a chance to reas-sert their true preferences. This reassertion takes place fairly quickly — as soon as owners of factors receive their increase incomes and spend them.*

It is unclear how we classify different categories of investments. What "layer" does a new apartment building fit into? The 3G wireless network buildout that drove the European telecom industry to near bankruptcy around the year 2000?

In practice, Austrian commentators in finance interpret malinvestment loosely, and it corresponds to whatever class of investments they feel are unjustified. Given the rather unhinged investment fads that investment banks have birthed, it is not difficult to find candidates for malinvestment.

Comparison to Other Schools of Thought

Ultimately, we end up with a story that cannot be practically distinguished from using a standard investment accelerator model (Section 4.4). The key difference appears to be the discussion of the role of interest rates, but it is somewhat difficult to put a very precise description on what their effect is. (In practice, popular Austrians mainly complain about central bankers "de-stroying price discovery in markets," which is a content-free statement.)

When we compare Austrian theory to neoclassical economics, politics is less of an issue. However, the investment accelerator logic is harder to reproduce within standard equilibrium-based models. In my view, this explains the greater visibility of Austrian economics within finance than you would expect given the fact that it has all but disappeared from the academic scene. The malinvestment logic fits the biases of finance professionals.

If we want to move past the basic investment-accelerator model, we need to discuss recent Austrian research. For example, there exists a literature of agent-based models found in Austrian economics journals. However, once we start looking at the mathematical models – and not the textual commentary – we are likely to end up with a mathematical convergence to similar post-Keynesian agent-based models. After all, if you slap together a bunch of agents into a mathematical model, the model behaviour is not going to depend on the backstory you apply to the model.

In conclusion, the literary approach to Austrian economics is very distinct from other schools of thought. However, that distinctiveness appears to fade if we attempt to express the ideas in formal models. That said, the deep ideological gulf between the Austrians and post-Keynesians probably means that both groups will largely ignore each other.

5.7   Conclusions

The heterodox explanation for most recessions can be viewed as a combination of two accelerator mechanisms: one created by investment (fixed investment and inventory), the other created by financial practices. Since investment normally requires external financing, we cannot easily disentangle these two mechanisms.

We can use national accounting identities – such as the Kalecki Profit Equation – to tie investment trends to profits and growth. We can also see that investment trends move in a pro-cyclical fashion. This means that we should expect most recessions to coincide with slumps in investment.

However, tying this view to recession forecasting is awkward. Investment trends are typically coincident with GDP growth, and so it does not directly give us a forecasting tool.

If we look at empirical recession models, yield curve slopes are typically the most reliable component. The question is why this is the case.

The second volume of this work will focus on interest rates and the cycle, including a deep dive in neoclassical business cycle theory (for which interest rates are a dominant factor).

Looking ahead to the arguments in that volume, the housing market is now a key component of fixed investment. Furthermore, the moves to deregulate housing finance in most developed countries have made the financing conditions for mortgages more cyclical. Therefore, it is no surprise that housing markets have been behind many of the recent recessions. This ties together the two legs of the post-Keynesian analysis of recessions, but the action is happening within the household sector, which was not normally the focus of traditional post-Keynesian models.

Finally, the linkage between finance and real investment puts recession forecasting into a fog of uncertainty. We might hope to be able to get a grip on slow-moving economic time series, but forecasting markets is quite obviously a different story. Even if one disputes the notion of market efficiency, it is clear that it is not easy to set up models that predict which way financial markets will move next (as otherwise, everyone would have already done it, and all investment managers would beat the market).

Data Sources

This text relies upon data that has come from a variety of sources. If the data is not from a national statistical agency, the source is indicated in the associated text. Figures list the data sources used (in abbreviated form). Further details on national sources follow.

- **Global.** The DB.nomics data platform is used for many international sources of data.
- **Canada.** Canadian data used was either calculated by Statistics Canada or the Bank of Canada. All data have been downloaded from the CANSIM delivery platform. URL: http://www5.statcan.gc.ca/cansim/home-accueil?lang=eng&p2=50&HPA
- **United States.** The United States has a number of agencies that generate statistical data. I most commonly use the Bureau of Economic Analysis (BEA) as well as the Bureau of Labor Statistics (BLS). For most of these sources, I download the data from the Federal Reserve Economic Data (FRED) website, which is a service provided by the St. Louis Federal Reserve Bank. (Other sources for U.S. data are noted below.) URL: http://research.stlouisfed.org/fred2/
- **United States Flow of Funds.** This is the Z.1 release, which is calculated by the Board of Governors of the Federal Reserve System. It is a comprehensive database of stocks and flows of financial assets. Given the number of series involved, it is easier to download the entire block of Z.1 data than on a series-by-series basis from FRED. URL: http://www.federalreserve.gov/releases/z1/
- **IMF.** The IMF publishes World Economic Outlook (WEO) databases, which contains historical data as well as forecasts. One of the advantages of these data is that they are presented using a consistent set of national accounting concepts. URL: https://www.imf.org/external/ns/cs.aspx?id=28
- **Japanese Ministry of Finance.** The Ministry of Finance (MoF) has a number of databases, including bond yields. URL: http://

www.mof.go.jp/english/jgbs/reference/interest_rate/index.htm
Calculations and plotting are done in the R computer language. Plots are generated using the *ggplot2* package.

References and Further Reading

References to articles and books appear within the endnotes of this report. The following list of books is of interest for understanding the post-Keynesian approach. (I refer to a few of my own books, which are listed at the end of this book.)

- *The Stock-Flow Consistent Approach: Selected Writings of Wynne Godley* (edited by Marc Lavoie, Gennaro Zezza), Palgrave Macmillan (2012). ISBN: 978-0-230-29311-3.
- *Monetary Economics: An Integrated Approach to Credit, Money Income, Production and Wealth (Second Edition)*, Wynne Godley and Marc Lavoie. Palgrave Macmillan, 2012. ISBN: 978-0-230-30184-9.
- *Post-Keynesian Economics: New Foundations*, by Marc Lavoie 2014. Edward Elgar, 2014. ISBN: 978-1-78347-582-7.
- *Can "It" Happen Again? Essays on Instability and Finance*, by Hyman P. Minsky, M.E. Sharpe, Inc., 1984. ISBN: 0-87332-213-4.
- *Why Minsky Matters: An Introduction to the Work of a Maverick Economist* by L. Randall Wray, Princeton University Press, 2016. ISBN: 978-0-691-15912-6
- *Debunking Economics – Revised, Expanded and Integrated Edition: The Naked Emperor Dethroned?*, by Steve Keen, Zed Books Ltd, 2011. ISBN: 8791780322209.
- *Golden Fetters: The Gold Standard and the Great Depression 1919-1939*, by Barry Eichengreen, Oxford University Press, 1992. ISBN: 0-19-510113-8.

About the Author

Brian Romanchuk founded BondEconomics.com in 2013, a website dedicated to providing analytical tools for the understanding of bond markets and monetary economics.

Previously, he was a senior fixed income analyst at *la Caisse de dépôt et placement du Québec* from 2006-2013, where he held a few positions, including being the head of quantitative analysis for fixed income. From 1998-2005, he worked as a quantitative analyst at BCA Research, a Montréal-based economic-financial research consultancy. During his time there, he developed a number of proprietary models for fixed income analysis, as well as covering the economies of a few developed countries.

Brian received a Ph.D. in Control Systems Engineering from the University of Cambridge, and held post-doctoral positions there and at McGill University. His undergraduate degree was in electrical engineering, from McGill. He is a CFA charter holder.

Brian currently lives in the greater Montréal area.

Also by BondEconomics

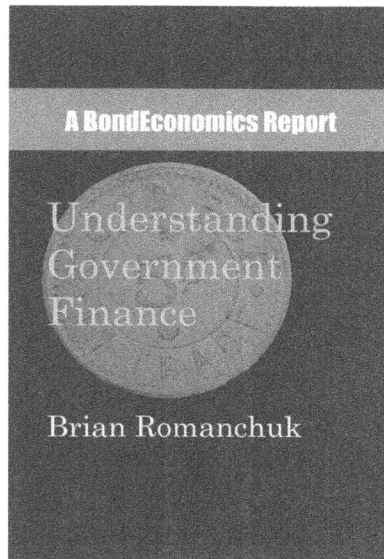

Understanding Government Finance (June 2015)
The government budget is not like a household budget. This report introduces the financial operations used by a central government with a free-floating currency, and explains how they differ from that of a household or corporation. The focus is on the types of constraints such a government faces.

This report introduces a simplified framework for the monetary system, along with the operating procedures that are associated with it. Some of the complications seen in real-world government finance are then added onto this simplified framework.

This report also acts as an introduction to some of the concepts used by Modern Monetary Theory, a school of thought within economics. Modern Monetary Theory emphasises the real limits of government action, as opposed to purely theoretical views about fiscal policy.

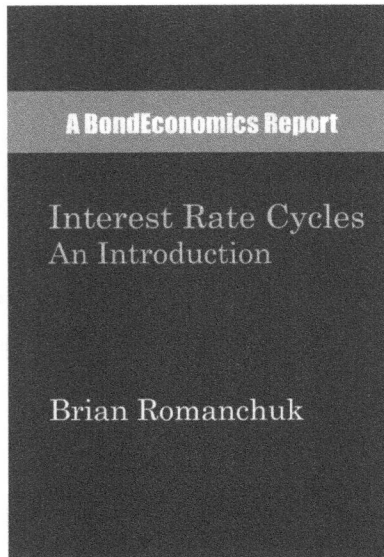

Interest Rate Cycles: An Introduction (June 2016)
Monetary policy has increasingly become the focus of economists and investors. This report describes the factors driving interest rates across the economic cycle. Written by an experienced fixed income analyst, it explains in straightforward terms the theory that lies behind central bank thinking. Although monetary theory appears complex and highly mathematical, the text explains how decisions still end up being based upon qualitative views about the state of the economy. The text makes heavy use of charts of historical data to illustrate economic concepts and modern monetary history. The report is informal, but contains references and suggestions for further reading.

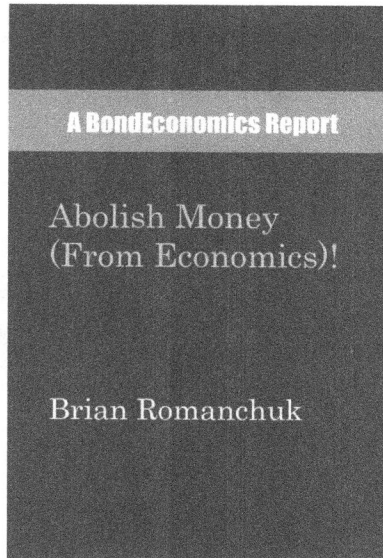

Abolish Money (From Economics)! (January 2017)

We live in a monetary economy, so it is not surprising that money plays an important role within economic theory. The argument of this book is that this role has become too important, and has warped our ability to think about the economy. The important psychological role of money within society has been transferred to monetary aggregates, and they are given far more significance than they deserve. Economists have wasted considerable time discussing reforms to the monetary system, such as Quantitative Easing, Positive Money, and Helicopter Money. We need to instead focus our attention on non-monetary reforms. This book consists of 22 essays that discuss the role of money within economic theory, and the controversies raised by debates about the role of money. The tone is informal, as the theoretical debates are translated into plain language.

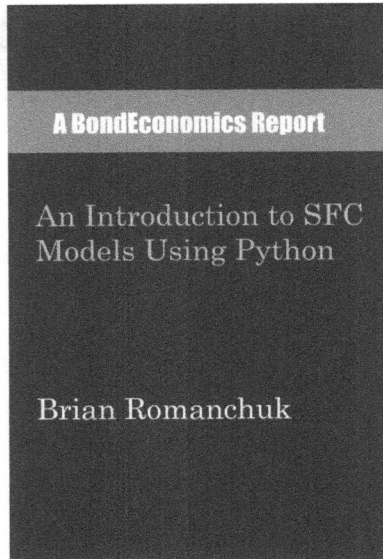

An Introduction to SFC Models Using Python (November 2017)
Stock-Flow Consistent (SFC) models are a preferred way to present economic models in the post-Keynesian tradition. This book gives an overview of the sfc_models package, which implements SFC models in Python. The approach is novel, in that the user only specifies the high-level parameters of the economic model, and the framework generates and solves the implied equations. The framework is open source, and is aimed at both researchers and those with less experience with economic models. This book explains to researchers how to extend the sfc_models framework to implement advanced models. For those who are new to SFC models, the book explains some of the basic principles behind these models, and it is possible for the reader to run example code (which is packaged with the software online) to examine the model output.

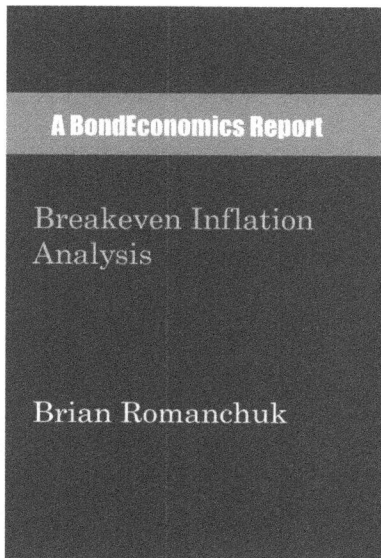

Breakeven Inflation Analysis (November 2018)
The great inflation of the 1970s in the developed countries provoked strong economic (and political) reactions. In finance, investors searched for ways to protect themselves from inflation. The United Kingdom launched the first modern inflation-linked bonds in 1981. In addition to being of interest to investors looking for protection against inflation, these bonds also provide a market-based measure of inflation expectations. Since investors have "skin in the game," the resulting forecasts might be better than a purely survey-based inflation forecast. More reliable inflation forecasts should be useful for policymakers that aim to control inflation.

Index